The finest thing we can experience is the mysterious. It is the fundamental emotion which stands at the cradle of true art and true science.

— Albert Einstein

Knowledge, Teaching and the Death of the Mysterious

*Six lectures given at
the West Coast Waldorf Teachers Conference
February 20–24, 2000*

Dennis Klocek

RSCP

The publisher is grateful for the encouragement and support of Robert Dulaney in making this publication possible.

© Copyright 2000 Dennis Klocek and Rudolf Steiner College Press

Art Work: Dennis Klocek
Cover Design: Claude Julien, Theodore Mahle and Hallie Wootan

ISBN 0-945803-54-0

The content of this book represents the view of the author and should in no way be taken as the official opinion or policy of Rudolf Steiner College or Rudolf Steiner College Press.

All Rights Reserved. No part of this book may be copied in any form whatsoever without the written consent of the publisher.

Book orders may be made through Rudolf Steiner College Bookstore. Tel. 916-961-8729, FAX 916-961-3032.

Rudolf Steiner College Press
9200 Fair Oaks Boulevard
Fair Oaks, CA 95628, U.S.A.

to the warrior spirit of Robert Musci

To the reader:

These lectures were given to teachers who are familiar with Rudolf Steiner's worldview and terminology. The reader who does not have such a background is referred to: *Creativity in Education: The Waldorf Approach* by René Querido; *Rhythms of Learning: What Waldorf Education Offers Children, Parents and Teachers,* edited by Roberto Trostli; or one of the books by Rudolf Steiner and many other authors included in the *Waldorf Education and Curriculum Resource Guide* available from Rudolf Steiner College Bookstore 916-961-8729 (Fax 916-961-3032).

Table of Contents

Introduction to Child Development 1

The Young Child from Birth to Seven 23

The Child from Seven to Fourteen 41

The Adolescent from Fourteen to Twenty-one 61

Adult Education 79

Development of the Heart-eye 99

Appendices 119

References 133

Introduction to Child Development

Lecture given February 20, 2000

When the conference committee asked me to give these lectures, I felt very thankful for the opportunity to speak to the teachers, because over the years I have been privy to conversations about all levels of educational work. My wife is a kindergarten teacher who gives me perspectives of the kindergarten work. I've worked in the high school here in Sacramento. I've worked in the lower school. I've taught adults most of my own adult life. It seems to me that the richness of the curriculum in the Waldorf school, and the richness of the work of Rudolf Steiner, have given us tremendous gifts. At the same time, because of the complexity of the curriculum, these insights bring a requirement that we be ever more precise when we speak to each other about the inner development of children—or, we could say, about the inner development of the human being. Often in a meeting where there are high school teachers and kindergarten teachers together, someone will say "the astral body of the young child." To a high school teacher, I would imagine that an image would arise of a twelve year old. What would arise in the consciousness of a kindergarten teacher is a picture of someone maybe about age four or five. And yet, the phrase, "the astral body of the young child," would be brought out as an illustration of a particular point, and then we would think we had communicated—or that we were both communicating the same idea, anthroposophically. I've seen this again and again.

So when I was asked by the committee if I would consider speaking, what immediately came to me was to try to form for you who are engaged in this sacred work of education with children, a kind of lexicon or a primer. I thought of taking the central theme of the book *Balance in Teaching*, and of going through the medical lectures, the biodynamic lectures, work on inner development and meditation, and Rudolf Steiner's whole oeuvre. I was looking, not for definitions necessarily, but for ways in which he has characterized these various bodies in the different developmental stages. I want to present them to you as a kind of leitmotif of the educational dialogue. In order for people at the college level to have a dialogue with people at the high school level or the middle school level, it seems to me that there needs to be a much more precise awareness. When we say something like "the astral body of the child," we really need to qualify what we are saying. I think that the Waldorf critics out in the world are bringing to Waldorf circles a challenge about our language. We need to be aware that there is a scientific rigor in Rudolf Steiner's work that falls through the cracks when we don't communicate to each other clearly about the appropriate developmental stages. So I set a task for myself to go through about ten different texts that I thought were applicable, and to try to bring together a meaningful boiling down of the work.

Each day of the conference I will go through a particular developmental stage. Today we'll do the pre-natal stage and try to see if there are common images and pictures that we can apply as a kind of a litmus test, so that we can say to ourselves: Yes, I am speaking about this kind of principle when I say "astral body" or "etheric body."

To do that I would like to start with the fundamental text, which is *Occult Science: an Outline*. In your packet that you were given for registration, there is a sheet that has an outline of the first Old Saturn stage, and at the bottom there are some embryological pictures (see below). The reason I put it on a handout is that the reality it represents is very complex, and I didn't want you to leave with the feeling of being overwhelmed. However, there are pictorial motifs that are very clearly given in this seminal work of Rudolf Steiner's that go on and on like fugues throughout his entire life. He keeps returning to them again and again, not necessarily with the same terminology, but with the same pictorial rigor. Since the task of the Waldorf teacher is to take very abstract things and make them pictorial, I thought that I would give us a little map of the territory. I don't propose to burden you with details, but I think that there are some things in these pictures, especially in the ordering of the pictures and the metamorphosis of the beinghood that he is describing in this work, that are very applicable to the developmental stages of a child.

At the top of the diagram you will see that there is a dotted circle, and in the center it says "Thrones."

On Old Saturn the first beings that Rudolf Steiner describes are the Thrones. He says they are beings who are composed of pure will. If you search through that work, he characterizes will in the following way:

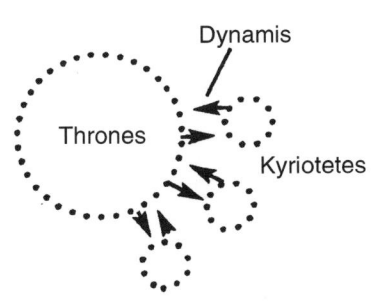

Will is to be completely, inwardly conscious of one's own being. Will enables a being to be completely conscious of its own being without any reference to an external being.

Now that's an interesting picture, because we normally think of will as something that is dissipated and spread out, as it is when we are straining to do something. But here, the picture of the will is the most intense self-awareness that could be possible. Self-awareness to the nth degree—that is a Throne—a completely self-aware being, a being of will. The pictorial gesture of this is what we could call a *relative center*.

In *Occult Science,* Rudolf Steiner goes on to describe that the Thrones, indeed, embody the quality of relative centers of warmth. So the picture of Thrones—if we could even try to imagine pictorially beings so exalted—would be that they were so aware of themselves that they created a kind of focal point of warmth. In that, there was a tremendous creative deed—the sacrificial deed of bestowing the substance of that self-awareness. In order for that substance of self-awareness to be understood or recognized, Rudolf Steiner gives a picture that there are beings, Kyriotetes, who see this deed from the periphery of creation and reflect this will back in to the center from the periphery. He calls those beings Kyriotetes, or Spirits of Wisdom, or—in his language in that particular work *(Occult Science)* cosmic intelligence.

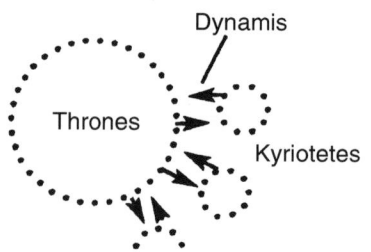

Here we have a leitmotif, a picture of a relative center raying out, being received by beings at a periphery who, in turn, reflect this force back in towards the relative center. In the center we have beings who are totally self-aware, and on the periphery the Kyriotetes are described as beings who are aware of others. What the Kyriotetes are aware of is the beings of the center. They are aware of others, whereas the beings of the center are aware of themselves. So right there, between the two beings, the Thrones and the Kyriotetes, we have a leitmotif of what later in other places Rudolf Steiner describes as the archetype of the human Ego.

In *The World of the Senses and the World of the Spirit*, there is a very vivid description that the original intention of the Gods was to create the human Ego in such a way that the Ego would oscillate between being aware of itself—awakening and lighting up with self-awareness—and, in that moment, being aware of all other beings who possessed the capacity to be aware of themselves. It would oscillate between recognizing the I AM in other beings, and then recognizing the I AM in itself, and then recognizing the I AM in the other being. This is the archetype of the human Ego. On Old Saturn, we have an oscillation happening between the Kyriotetes and the Thrones much like this, but really there are no other created beings who are there to be aware of both the Kyriotetes and the Thrones. The Thrones are aware of themselves, and the Kyriotetes are aware of the Thrones. So then what?

What happens is that there are other beings who arise in the movement of consciousness between the Thrones and the Kyriotetes. They, appropriately, are the Spirits of Movement, the Dynamis.

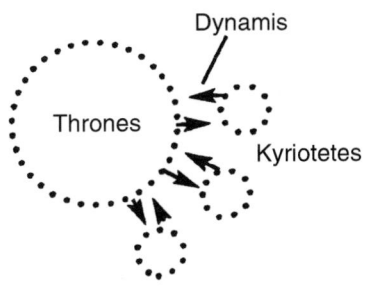

Those Spirits of Movement, in the diagram, are the little arrows between the Kyriotetes and the Thrones. And what the Dynamis are aware of is the way in which the will of the Thrones plays into the wisdom of the Kyriotetes, and the way in which the wisdom of the Kyriotetes is reflected back into the will impulses of the Thrones. The Dynamis represent a middle being who is aware of the play and the motion and the revelation of these forces. Now this middle being, the one who arises in the middle, is really another great archetype of the human Ego. We could say that the Dynamis are an image of the second member of the Trinity, the one in between, the one who is aware of all, the one who unites the two polarities. In the Spirits of Motion we have a kind of intermediary force that can be either awakening in itself, or awakening in the other, a kind of oscillatory movement that is happening between these two poles of consciousness.

Now we have the first three actors, so to speak, on the stage, and that motif of awakening in the self, then awakening in the other, then being aware of the awakening in the other, then awakening in the self being aware, is really the lot of what eventually will be the path of self development in the human being. The human being is continually in the act of becoming. The human being is the one in between, who finds a kind of independent place in the whole creation of the cosmos, where neither the world of the senses nor the world of the spirit has an impact. It is in another realm, a purely human realm, that exists in between. It's that purely human realm which is the great gift of the human, and also the great challenge. That is really the focus of the work in education, because in that realm there is the arising of what later we will come to call the astral principle. It's in that middle realm where the challenge to the individuality arises.

Let's look at the embryology diagram of the first nine days of human life. What I'm going to try to do for you in these next days is to present to you pictures out of embryology and the evolution of the four meteorological organs—the liver, the lung, the kidney, and the heart—as characteristic of the developmental stages from childhood into the sentient soul period from twenty-one to twenty-eight. Each seven-year period has a characteristic organ that it relies upon, so to speak, in order to make the consciousness of the child at that particular stage appear in the soul in a particular way. For example, when you work in the middle school, you are really dealing with children who are being impacted very strongly by their lung forces. It is often the case that, when receiving a first grade class, if the teachers are having problems with the children, the teachers will experience pneumonia themselves. The children around them are going through the Fall from Paradise, and the place where the children are experiencing that is in their lungs. There are many things we can look at in the embryology of a particular organ that give a picture of the developmental stage and the readiness of a particular level of consciousness, of a kindergartener or of a middle school child. They are looking at the world, we could say, *through* an organ. It is useful for the teacher to know this. But if we want to look for a leitmotif, let's look before there are even organs.

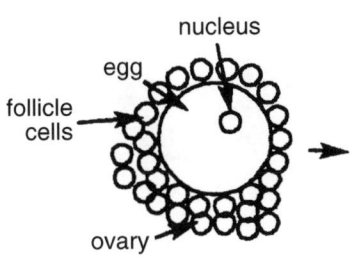

Let's look right at the very beginning—in the ovary of a woman. That first little figure is the diagram from *Gray's Anatomy* of an ovum, an egg, in the ovary—surrounded by the cells of the ovary. What we can see is that the cells of the ovary have a very strange resemblance to the Kyriotetes, and the ovum itself has a very interesting relationship to the picture of the Thrones. The ovum is, we could say, self-aware. The ovary and the cells of the ovary are a kind of reflection, as cells, of this giant cell somehow growing in its midst. That is the condition of all of the thousands and thousands of egg cells that are in an ovary in a woman at the time of her own birth. When a woman is born, she has a complete complement of all the eggs that could ever be used, and they are all in this paradisical situation, where they all are very large cells. They are the largest cells in the body, surrounded by a kind of aura of other cells whereby they get their nutrition and their support. It is all there microscopically in the ovaries, even of an embryo. Even as a fetus, the woman has actually many, many eggs and, as she is born, a lot of them slough off till there are just a couple thousand in there. Here is a process of small cells surrounding a larger cell, and we see what Rudolf Steiner calls an *anlagen,* a prophetic form, an analogous form. The term *anlagen* is German, but it actually is used in embryological texts to describe these organs that form in an embryo, which are pointing towards a later development. It's a very interesting idea. Rudolf Steiner uses it very often in describing soul qualities.

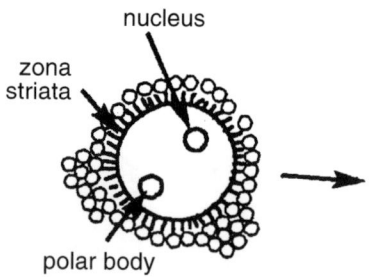

If we look at the second diagram of the embryology of the first nine days, we see that something has happened. Within that egg, down at the bottom, there is a polar body; it's another little circle. The nucleus divides in two, and the DNA separates so that each egg will have only half the chromosomes. The polar body forms there. At the same time, the *zona striata* forms around the egg. That *zona striata* is a zone that forms in between, where there are no cells. There is just a movement between the cells on the outside and the egg. A kind of fluid motion goes between the two, but there is no cellular structure there. Also what is known as the *zona pellucida* is a similar non-cellular form where there is movement back and forth of fluids. In that we can see a leitmotif of the Dynamis.

Here, in the formation of the egg cells within an ovary, we have an analogous form to that of Old Saturn. As the *zona striata* forms, in the upper diagram we see that, under the Exusiai, the generalized motions form agglomerations of antipathetic and sympathetic qualities, which gives the body of Saturn the quality of being composed of small individualized parts. What happens in the next phase of the egg's development, when the *zona striata* forms, is that the interior of the egg begins to shape itself into something resembling a mulberry. Parts begin to individualize; they separate out from the nucleus. The egg starts to organize itself into a structure with inner forms. This is very much the gesture of what later will be called the *astral principle*.

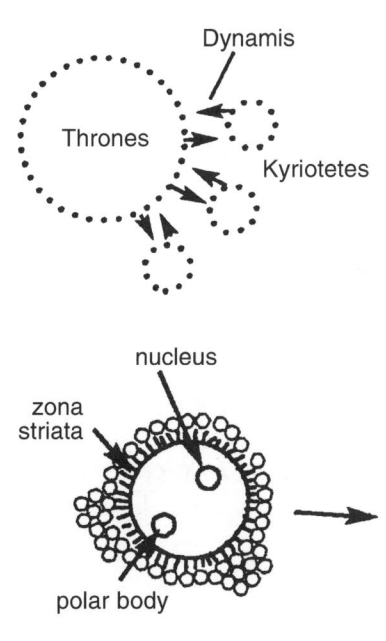

In the astral principle, something comes out of the *general* life of the organism and forms a little separate *inner* zone where something else can happen. This is the cause of illness in the biological spheres. Something forms out of the general life of the organism and creates an inner, cyst-like formation. The Exusiai on Old Saturn represent an evolution following the first evolution of Thrones, Kyriotetes, and Dynamis—with the center and the periphery and motion in between. Suddenly the next thing that happens on Old Saturn is that the Exusiai form a little mulberry on the inside of Old Saturn. That's exactly what happens after the *zona striata* forms in the egg.

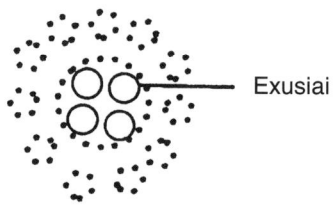

Now in the embryology, we can see that in the next stage of evolution something very unusual happens. The mulberry form in the egg divides and divides. It is still inside the ovary and it differentiates into various polar bodies. Then the whole form of the egg separates out so that there is a ring of cells around a follicle. This all happens in the ovary, culminating in a follicle that fills with fluid.

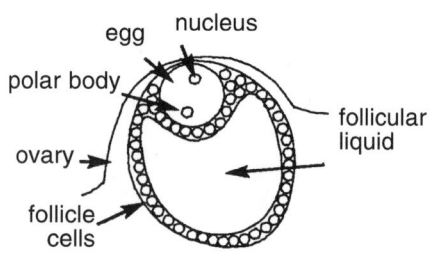

All of the contents that used to be the egg get pushed to one side near the surface of the ovary. The follicle fills with fluid and a pressure builds; it's like a pimple. The more the fluid fills the follicle, the more the egg is pushed towards the surface until eventually the surface erupts and the egg is ejected from a little pocket in the wall of the ovary into the fallopian tube. This is concurrent with the estrus cycle of the woman. That is when she is ovulating.

That picture of a hollow forming and then, within it, cells forming a kind of nucleus—that's really an image of the next phase on Old Saturn. If we look where the Archai, the Spirits of Personality, are forming what Rudolf Steiner calls a shell of warmth around Old Saturn, we see that within that shell of warmth the Archangeloi, or the Archangels, the Spirits of Fire, awaken within the Saturn body. They have the feeling: I exist because my environment allows me to exist.

The little egg cell is living amidst the pressure of the follicle growing in the ovary, creating a pressure on one side, and then on the other side, the great expanse of the unknown, outside of the ovary. 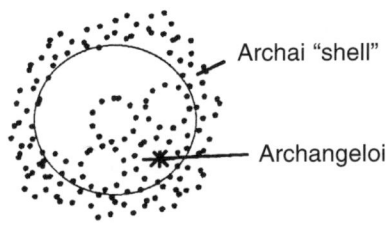 There is a tube going down into who-knows-where. We have the drama of the ejection of the moon about to happen. In planetary evolution, as soon as we get to the Archangels, things level out a little—and then there is a pralaya, and then the sun comes back. In *Occult Science: an Outline*, you can read about how the moon is ejected from the Earth. The erupting of the egg is a picture of that.

If we look at that as a motif, we see first the play between the center and the periphery, with the zone in between, and then a forming on the inside of a proliferating nucleus, and then the dividing again to the outside and the inside—the same motif that was there in the first stage. When that happens it is as if there is almost a recapitulation of the first stage already in Old Saturn.

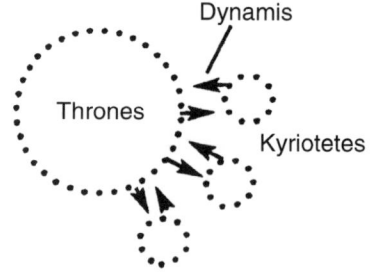

The first motif, where we have something in the center, something at the periphery, and something in the inside is repeated again by the Archangels and by the Archai. It is the same thing as we would find in reading the document, *Occult Science: an Outline*. It gets so confusing. We ask: What is happening here? But if we take that first motif as an image we see that there is something in the center; then there is something at the periphery which is recognizing what's in the center; then there's a motion between the periphery and the center, a kind of dialogue. Then what's in the center begins to proliferate.

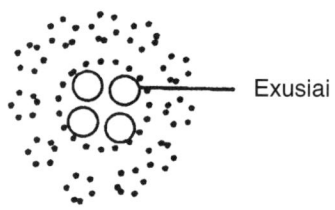

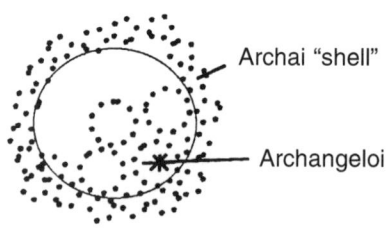

Then once again, a periphery, and then once again a center, and a periphery and a center and a periphery and a center. The image keeps repeating at each stage.

That is the fundamental motif of education. Here I am; I'm the student. There you are; you're the teacher. There you are; you're the student. Here I am; I'm the teacher. The dialogue, the motion, between the two souls from me to you and you to me—we call it education. There is a breathing. Every organ in the body is breathing between itself and its environment. Every cell is breathing between itself and the environment. All beings are breathing between themselves and their environments. It is the breathing of the organism, both the physical organism and the soul organism, that is really the focus of the educational enterprise. How can we keep the center and the periphery in dialogue with one another? If we can't keep the breathing going, if we can't allow the center to be open to the periphery, if we can't allow the periphery to reflect back what is happening in the center, if we can't get a rhythmic interplay between the two, if we can't establish a motion between the two, then the educational rhythm, the educational potential, is lost. It becomes too intellectual, or it becomes too Dionysian, too artistic. We don't have the proper balance between the two.

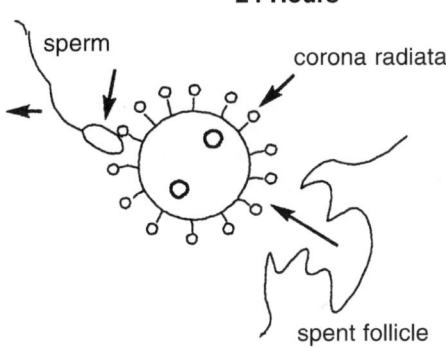

24 Hours

sperm

corona radiata

spent follicle

Now, about these themes of the center and the periphery that we find there on Old Saturn—if we skip to the egg at twenty-four hours after it comes out of the ovary, we see that it does exactly what happened back when it formed the *zona striata*. It forms what is known as the *corona radiata*. The diagram that shows the spent follicle is the ovary. The ovary ruptures. The egg is placed out into the void of the fallopian tube. It sprouts cells on little stalks around the outside—images of the Kyriotetes. There is a zone between those cells on the outside and the egg itself where there is a *lot* of chemistry going on. The reason why the chemistry is going on there is that there is something very interesting about to happen—the meeting with the sperm. Now the chemistry that is happening in that space between the *corona radiata* and the surface of the egg is there so that when that sperm touches the surface of the egg, the whole acidity-alkalinity balance of the area of the *corona radiata* totally shifts and will not allow any other sperm, no matter how close, to touch the surface of that egg. That center—between the cells of the *corona radiata* and the surface of the egg—becomes a sacred space. It becomes an inward space, where only *one* can be. This is the exact picture of the astral body. It's the one where I experience myself as ME. Right there where that sperm comes in and gives its content of chromosomes to that egg, there is a magical zone of motion—a picture of the Dynamis.

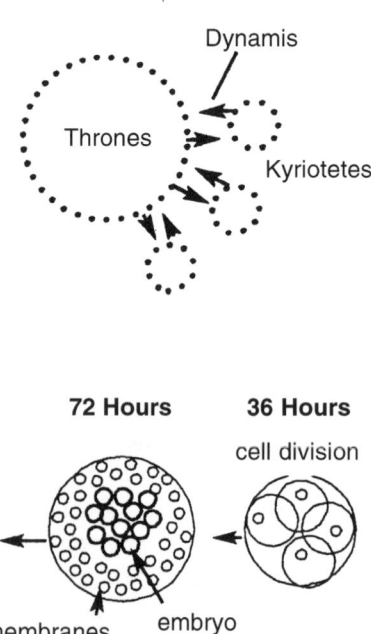

The first thing that happens is the Dynamis are once again at work. Thirty-six hours later the Exusiai have entered.

The chromosomes have given such a stimulus to *form* that the egg begins to replicate itself and make form after form. It exudes cells. This form impulse becomes so great that there is actually, at seventy-two hours, the first beginning of an embryo through a concentration of cells in the center (read: Archangeloi) and another zone of less concentrated cells which will eventually be the sheaths of the placenta.

So we have a germ disk forming Archangels. We have a zone on the outside that will be a sheath like the Archai—until, finally, in the same evolution that happened in the ejection of the egg from the ovary, forming the ovarian follicle, we have the same pattern repeating again, but this time it is the embedding of the fertilized egg into the wall of the uterus. The same type of follicular form unfolds in the blastocyst with its membranes and the placental membranes, with the germ disk at one end of the embryo with its various layers that start to form. It is exactly the same pattern.

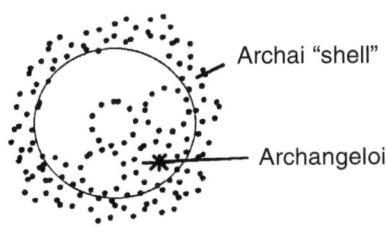

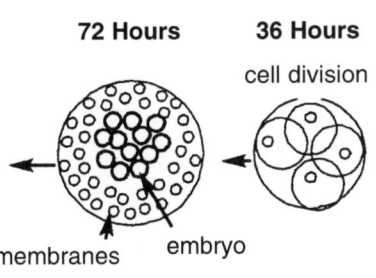

We could go on. This is just the first nine days out of nine months. If you were to take the time to actually look, you would see that this pattern is repeated endlessly, endlessly, endlessly

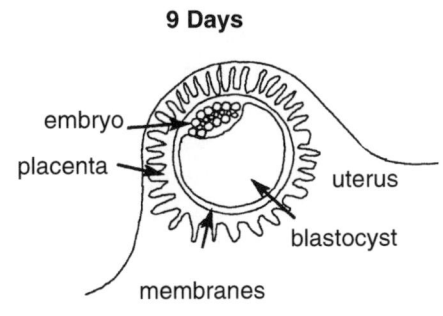

15

as a mantra in the formation of the biological forms of the embryo. When Rudolf Steiner is speaking out of his genius in this early work of *Occult Science*, the amazing thing to me is that very early on he was speaking these pictures very clearly, and through the rest of his life he was saying exactly the same things again and again and again. It is truly awesome the way he could see these archetypal pictures so early and then go back and give them in detail later in all the works on education and biodynamics and healing arts and medicine and so on.

So I offer these pictures to you as food for thought for what we could call the method of analogy. The great challenge of the Waldorf teacher is to be able to create living pictures out of abstract data in such a way that the pictures carry the intellectual content of the lesson as a pictorial unfolding process. What I've just done for you is to try to show you the analogous pictures of processes in *Gray's Anatomy* and *Occult Science: an Outline*. As you go to make a botany lesson or a physiology lesson, you encounter a tremendous wall of data that is dead. Somehow you have to bring it to children in a way that makes it living. Somehow the pictures have to be presented in such a way that the child doesn't turn off.

The master teachers will always bring living pictures because they worked hard and long to get them out of their own meditative life. What I would like to give you in these pictures is the idea that there are certain keys that you can learn to look for. In our meditative life we can actually take archetypal pictures—one of them is the Thrones and the Kyriotetes and the Dynamis on Old Saturn—and begin to work with that meditatively and apply that, as a kind of mantra, to our work in the sciences. If you can do that, you will find that the science lesson becomes very interesting for you, and that you can find appropriate pictures in the hard data which will begin to live in your soul so that, in your meditations, pictures start to come to you that are exactly what the class requires. You can find, in the data, pictures which are coming as questions from the children. The master teachers do this so well. The teachers who are struggling with the data may be going into fifth grade teaching—and they have never looked at a plant and suddenly they have to deal with botany. This can be difficult. The *pictorial*, in other words, the *way in which the picture moves,* is what I am trying to share with you. If you get that correct, things will go well.

Each day I will take today's diagram and move it a bit further, so we can see that, in the genius of Rudolf Steiner and the insight that he had into child development, there is a natural unfolding, just like this. There is a natural unfolding in the soul life—the drama of the incarnating ego.

The theme in child development is that, coming from the periphery there is a being who is trying to incarnate in a body of flesh. Since that being is not accustomed to living in a body of flesh, there are some adjustments that need to occur both ways, in order that the integration can unfold properly. The adjustments must happen in that middle realm, in the astral body. In *Fundamentals of Therapy*, Rudolf Steiner gives the picture that the astral body is the place where illness happens. In *Balance in Teaching*, Rudolf Steiner also places that gesture towards illness in the astral body, but he calls the astral principle the source of the building-up forces or the musical forces.

Now that sounds to me like a paradox. And yet, what we really need to understand is what he means when he says "etheric" and "astral," and that there is an etheric and an astral that is in the periphery, and there is an etheric and astral that is in the center. There is an earthly etheric and astral, and there is a cosmic etheric and astral. If I can just present that in the next couple days, that is the drama of the adolescent. That is the drama of the middle school child struggling against a gestating astral body.

The principle is that when a body is born in the soul life, the next developing body is going through its gestation. As that happens, the gestation creates a kind of turbulence in the soul so that the body that has just been born has to struggle with this gestation. When the physical body is born, the ether body is gestating, and it is that gestation of the ether body—which will be born at the seventh year at the change of teeth—that is creating a kind of turbulence, a kind of *anlagen*, of what is going to happen later on. So there are the terrible twos, and the pre-pre-pre-adolescent fives, and all these prophetic gestures that are present in child development. How could it be that a five year old is giving us a picture of adolescent rebellion? How is that? They don't have any sheaths for that, but it is already present as a kind of inner gestation.

That is the picture I want to present to you over the next couple days, because that picture helps to make sense of this astral-etheric flip-flop. There are certain parts of the astral body which never really incarnate, and certain parts of the astral body which the Ego grabs hold of and brings down into incarnation. The Ego focuses it and brings it down. Then it becomes problematic.

When we say "astral body," it is like saying "Fair Oaks" or something. There is a lot of real estate there. *Astral body* is a very generic term. *Etheric body* is a very generic term. It's my feeling that, if we become a little clearer with each other in our language, our critics will not have so much ammunition.

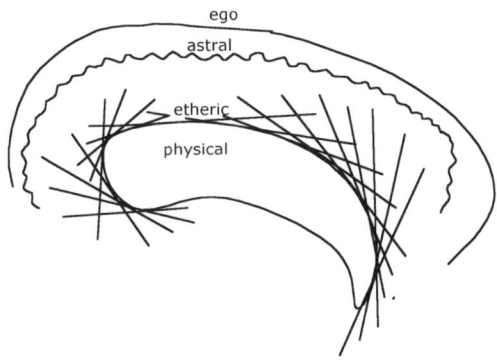

So. Here is a picture. This little kidney shape is the embryo, and the little lines around it are the sheaths of the placenta. In development, in gestation, what is happening in the embryo is that the *physical body* is gestating. It hasn't yet been born. The etheric is definitely present; it has to be there or there are no life forces. The astral is definitely present. It must be or there are no musical forces, or ordering forces, no harmony of the spheres. The Ego must be present or else there is no destiny pattern for the unfolding. There is nothing to guide the physical, from a higher place, through destiny forces of race and geography—something that must guide the destiny of this being. The Ego needs to be there, but the Ego is present in a form that we could call cosmic. Here I have written ego, but it is cosmic Ego. We could say that another name for cosmic Ego is *true being* or *true self*. It is a being that is, we could say, looking at the I AM. It is witnessing the I AM. Its whole life is spent looking towards the I AM. It is the transcendent destiny pattern from life to life to life to life.

That's Ego with a capital E. It will not incarnate as an actual viable principle until the twenty-first year. But it is present in the forming of the embryo as a cosmic reality. Its picture is the forming of the sheaths of the *zona striata*, or the *zona pellucida*, of this sheath-like interim space between the hierarchies and the mother. It is a kind of intermediary movement zone, where the highest destiny patterns come down and start to ray into what eventually will be the physical substance of the embryo. The Ego is there as a kind of outer movement zone. It is weaving through the sounding of the stars and the motions of the planets, moving in their loops, giving their organ-forming principles—the cosmic astral, the ordering principle, the musical principle, the principle that creates interval. Then, from the stars themselves, from the cosmic etheric, even beyond the planets, there are forces of life raying down. The cosmic etheric gives us forces of life. The cosmic astral gives us forces of order. The cosmic Ego gives us the true self.

Those three forces working from the cosmos, working together, provide the sheaths in which the embryo will grow. They work from the periphery: planar forces, etheric forces, form-building forces, forces of musical interval, forces of destiny, heredity—all streaming down and through the wonderful organ of the uterus, creating a field of activity—and, through time, after conception or even in conception, the Ego with its true self as a picture of the cosmic destiny going back through the Dynamis into the will impulse of the Thrones, the impulse to say I AM, I exist.

That being of the Ego brings some of the high celestial force from the hierarchies, that high cosmic sense of the I AM, and brings it down, down, down. A part of the Ego incarnates with the physical, as a representative of the highest cosmic spirit force coming right down into matter. That little germ there of the physical actually starting to create a vessel into which life can incarnate, into which a soul can incarnate and eventually an ego—that's right there in the very beginning when a part of the cosmic Ego separates off and comes down and connects down into the physical body.

We could almost say *physical ego,* or an *ego image*—a seed, an ego seed in the actual physical.

That seed of that Ego is present in the human sense organs. It is through the sense organs that the embryo is receiving all these other astral and etheric and Ego forces—through the sensing of the pressures and the sounds and the temperatures and the fluid motions in the womb. The Ego provides for this young being the organs on the periphery, in the skin and in the nerves, to receive all of these forces through the intra-uterine sheaths, and forms a vessel, a creative space in the center, into which a being can incarnate. In the coming days I will try to show you how the astral body, at a certain stage—a part of it—comes down and joins these others as the Ego pushes it down. The ether body gets pushed down by the Ego. The incarnating Ego keeps taking pieces and bringing them down, but as it brings them down and invests them in the being, it doesn't mean that the cosmic astral or the cosmic etheric are exhausted. There still are sheaths present.

We could ask: Why? When the being is finally formed and an ego finally incarnates in the flesh, it can then go the long and lonely road to consciously excarnate back into these cosmic sheaths to form a cosmic womb across the threshold. That then is the meditative life. That is the inner life of anthroposophy—the techniques that we use to try, now that we have incarnated, to turn back around and take our soul-spiritual and once again enter consciously as a true self—once again perceive the workings of the cosmic astral in our inner life, once again perceive the workings of the cosmic etheric in our very life forces, and to penetrate our sense organs with cognition in the transformation of the senses.

On the last day of the conference I would like to present to you the task of the adult educator. That is where I do most of my work. I will try to give a picture of this great challenge of the young people who are between twenty-one and twenty-eight who have gone through Waldorf schools and are now out in the world and have taken what you folks have given them. They now want to learn how to become citizens of the world with those gifts. It is a unique challenge there, in the twenty-one to twenty-eight group. My colleagues who work at Rudolf Steiner College can tell you that—especially for the Waldorf kids when they come back. They have a certain something that has been awakened in them—a tremendous ideal—and if we don't provide opportunities to go back once again into these cosmic realms consciously, then there is a great despair that arises out of their idealism. But more of that next Thursday.

The Young Child from Birth to Seven

Lecture given February 21, 2000

Today what I would like to address is a difficult subject in the work of Rudolf Steiner. We could say it is the question: What is the etheric? This is a difficult question because the birth of a child into the world, the birth of the physical body of a child, is accompanied by etheric forces from the cosmos that have been working through nine months to form a kind of cupola, a space, into which all of the patterns of organs and endocrine pathways, warmth and cold differentials, membranes, secretions—all of these very complex chemical reactions—have to be somehow coordinated and integrated in one space, with very little room for error. If we really think of the miracle of organization that it takes to bring an embryo to term, it is mind-boggling. Yet it is a daily occurrence. We look at this great miracle and almost take it for granted.

That process of the becoming of the human being from the nothing to the something is spearheaded and supported by the forces of the etheric. The whole being of the embryo is surrounded by cosmic Ego forces—forces of destiny, karma, heredity, entering a particular race, incarnating into a particular geographic area. All of those forces are a kind of filter

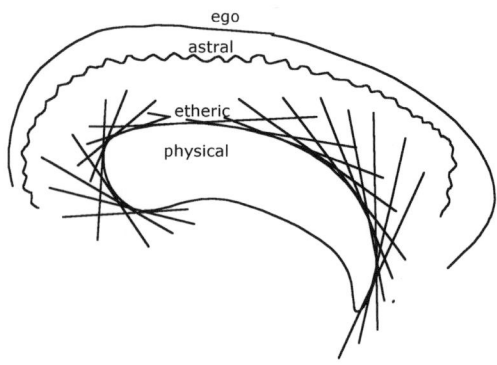

very far out in the cosmos, which we could call the Ego principle. The Ego could be thought of as a lens, but it is a selective lens that brings certain forces from the cosmos to bear in a center. It brings forces from the periphery and integrates them into what we could call a relative center. It does that primarily through the gates of the senses. The forming of the sense life in the environment of the embryo is really orchestrated by what later will be called the ego organization from the physical side or, from a cosmic side, the *true self*. The ego organization in the embryo is the actual physical response of matter to the organizing forces of the cosmos, but those physical responses are based on patterns of sensation that exist in potential in the farthest reaches of the cosmos. We could say that sensation is the raw material of the cosmos. No physiologist can really explain sensation in a mechanical/chemical model. Even though we know all of the instruments and the pathways that sensation takes in physiology, when it comes to the question in embryology of just how sensation forms the embryo, no one knows. But most agree that sensation does form the embryo.

There was an article in today's *Sacramento Bee* (see Appendix) about a new thesis that yes, neurons do grow. For many years it has been assumed that the human being comes in with a certain complement of neurons and that's it for the rest of life. It has been discovered that in songbirds, part of the brain actually atrophies every season so that a new song can be learned. It was considered that a human already had a full complement of neurons and that new neuronal patterns could not be developed. The researcher who determined that twenty years ago has now reversed his position. He now says, yes indeed, new neurons can be developed, even to old age, but it depends on the effects of the environment. This is cutting edge research, and this is exactly what Rudolf Steiner was saying years ago.

We could say that the Ego acts, through the gates of the twelve senses, as a kind of filter or lens for cosmic force. Inside that gate of the senses within the organism is found the action of the cosmic astral body, the motion of the planets—in front of the fixed stars—creating loops and pockets and angles and particular forms. Within that realm of the cosmic astral is what we could call the personal etheric, or the individualized etheric. It is these individualized etheric forces to which Rudolf Steiner is often referring when he uses the phrase *etheric formative forces*. They are the etheric forces which create form. The etheric forces themselves, per se, are really cosmic forces. According to Rudolf Steiner, if the human form were placed into the pure, cosmic etheric forces, it would be disintegrated; it would be annihilated.

Now this seems like a contradictory perspective—that in one instance the etheric forces would annihilate the human form, and from another perspective the etheric forces are there as the source of the sculptural forces, of the building of the form. It seems contradictory, until we develop a perspective that every "body" such as the Ego, the astral body, the etheric body—every subtle body—has a cosmic dimension and an earthly dimension. In the earthly dimension, these cosmic forces, which really live on the periphery of the cosmos, come under the spell, so to speak, of the Ego being and become focused into a relative center. From there these cosmic forces begin to create form. They begin to create the possibility of the upbuilding and maintaining of the form. The upbuilding of the form is the work of the musical forces.

The musical forces allow the *new* to have a place to manifest. The creation of the previously determined pattern of the form itself and its decay, we could say, are the work of the etheric forces. It is when the cosmic side of these celestial forces comes under the sway of an Ego being that the possibility of awakening in a body of flesh arises. The young child goes from existing as a spiritual being living among spiritual beings, that is as a cosmic Ego, and starts a journey through the stars and the planets, picking up impulses from the stars and planets that will eventually become the actual functions and forms within the human body. Human beings are on a journey towards incarnation. They take these celestial forces and, through the deeds of Lucifer and Ahriman, focus these celestial forces in a relative center to such a degree that an illusion of a separate self arises and is sustained.

This doesn't mean that the incarnated being no longer has a transcendent cosmic self. It just means that the illusion of the separate self has become so focused by the Ego being that the adversaries have gained access to it through the door of matter. The matter gets incorporated into these celestial forces as an image of particular regions of the cosmos in the lung and the liver and the kidney and the heart and the bones and the senses and all of the interaction between the life organs and the sense organs. This all gives the human being the possibility of becoming another small universe. The potential human has a full compliment of cosmic forces, but they have been individualized to the degree that the being who is occupying this new body has the distinct impression that he or she is the center of the universe.

There is nothing wrong with this except that the original plan was that, as soon as this perception arose, the human being would immediately have the complementary perception that our intrinsic uniqueness is what we have in common with every other being that says "I." According to Rudolf Steiner, that was the original plan. The function of a human being was to oscillate between those two states of consciousness as a kind of reciprocating relief valve between the cosmos and the Earth, to allow for a breathing between a peripheral cosmos and a centric cosmos. The ether body of the child, under the influence of the incarnating Ego at the physical birth, becomes a kind of lens or focalizing agent that takes part of the cosmic ether—the stars we could say, or the light of the stars—and gathers the qualities of earth, water, air, and fire that exist in the various constellations. As the sun moves through the zodiac, it brings, month by month, the successive qualities of earth, water, air, and fire into the ethers around the earth. The incarnating Ego, which is an image of the sun moving through the cosmos, focuses into a relative center in the embryo a field of forces which the embryo participates in for nine months. The other three months that are left over, we could say, are the reason why we come back—because we can't really have the whole picture of the whole cosmos in one incarnation. Then when we do come back, we will have another three points of view we haven't quite worked out for each incarnation.

The activity of the Ego which brings a whole starry realm into focus, also brings a focus into the other subtle bodies. In the other subtle bodies the individualized etheric forces could be called earthly etheric forces, or personal etheric forces. Those personal etheric forces have the property of being plant-like. Plants have two fundamental modes of action: they grow and then they decay. Growth and decay are the properties of life. Life grows by adding one and adding one and adding one. That is growth. The paradox is that life also *decays* by adding one and adding one and adding one. This is because if we keep adding and adding and adding, suddenly the physical dimensions of the being exceed its ability to maintain the integrity of the life.

This is called the *law of minimal surfaces* in physics. What it means is, if you get too big, you have to get broken apart. Think of a balloon. We fill a balloon; we keep filling a balloon; we keep filling a balloon. As we keep filling the balloon, we're just filling the balloon. We're doing the same thing; we are growing. But suddenly something happens. As the mass of the being grows by cubes (3 dimensions), the surface is only growing by squares (2 dimensions), and something has got to give. The surface membrane ruptures, and the organism goes back to a more economical stage; the organism forms a committee. Instead of trying to solve everything in the College of Teachers, we form committees, and we mandate them to grow. It is exactly the same process. All that is happening in the social life is the law of minimal surfaces.

In the biological sphere, this limits the size of the growth of a particular cell. The cell of an elephant or a whale is the same size as the cell of a mouse; there is no difference. There are just more of them. The size of a cell is limited by its ability to maintain integrity between the center of the cell and the periphery of the cell. This image of the Thrones (the Spirits of Will), the Kyriotetes, and the Spirits of Motion again. There is just so much growth that can happen inside a cell, until the membrane has to rupture and then the cell goes through a process to reform into a smaller size, as two cells. There you have the Exusiai again. Then the cell can maintain integrity. These are images that we could call the laws of the etheric, and they govern everything from individual cells in your body to governments and social revolutions. They are images of the same principles, and they come from the first phase of evolution on Old Saturn.

In Rudolf Steiner's teachings, the etheric forces have two parameters. One is that they bring life forces, forces of growth, from the periphery.

In the diagram above, I've drawn a circle, made of lines, that represents what Rudolf Steiner calls the planar forces of the etheric realm. He says that the ether forces come to the organism as planes of light from the periphery. The life comes to the organism from the periphery, from the cosmos. The growth also comes to the organism from the periphery. But within the transformed ether body of etheric formative forces, these growth forces have become so individualized that they link themselves up to the physical properties of the matter that gets incorporated into them. What results from the originally cosmic growth forces is that suddenly matter falls out of the now individualized growth forces, like the wake of a ship. There is a kind of turbulence. As the growth forces form a space, matter goes into the space and fills it up. Then what is left is matter, and the growth forces withdraw to the periphery to create another layer of life in which matter can manifest. This is the way a tree grows—from the cambium. The cambium is on the periphery; that is where the life is.

In the human organism, on the periphery are the senses: the eyes and the ears and the skin and the touching. The life forces—through the senses, through the sensation—come into the young child from the periphery—star light pouring through the gates of the senses. This is cosmic life. The forces—cosmic life—form the organs in cosmic star patterns of earth and water and air and fire; they form the lung, liver, kidney, heart. The particular pattern of the particular organ is a picture of the way in which the elements are working in that particular realm. The lung is a picture of the earth, the way in which the carbon of the earth unites with substances and then dissolves, for instance. These life forces from the periphery come in contact with young children through the environment, through what they hear and what they see and what they touch and what they taste. The moods of the other beings (adults) around the children also carry these life forces in the sheaths that are around them (adults). Young children have a kind of atavistic clairvoyance as to how humans or animals have organized these cosmic forces. They don't listen so much to the content of a speaker's voice but to the intent, to the elemental mood of the speaker. They look at the way in which the curves in the speaker's face are animated or not, the way in which their limbs reflect their inner mobility, and from there they build their own organs from birth to seven. This is an enormous thought, that what is in the environment of a child from birth to seven is what is actually forming their life organs, through the gates of the senses. These life organs are nourished by sense impressions from the environment.

Now, in the child from birth to seven, the physical body has been born and the ether body has been pulled by the Ego into the physical body, but the ether body hasn't yet been freed. It is still working in a rather cosmic way. It is gestating, we could say, in the child from birth to seven. It is mulling over the impressions, the life impressions, that are coming in, and forming the inner organs according to the dictates of the cosmos: Now you must form a liver. Now you must form a lung. Now you must form a heart. And we could think that those organs are created in the embryo and finished, but no. They are seed-like in the fetus that has come to term. They are still unfolding. They need earth evolution in order to actually experience how the cosmic ether forces have come through the realm of the planets and are actually forming and creating the earthly forms of the body. This process is an initiation that the young children are going through before the change of teeth so that, later on, when they pick up their karma-designated temperament, when the ether body is born, they will be able to take a particular temperament on for a time and then let go of it in order to integrate it into the other temperaments. They need to have an initiation in the school of the elemental beings.

The elemental initiation they have is the forming of their life organs as a gestation process in the period from birth to seven. That initiation is through the sensations that they receive from their environment. As a result, their educative principle is imitation. They imitate what is in the environment around them. Teaching through example is the most effective form of education for birth to seven, because this is the biological imperative of that age. The etheric formative forces are impacting the physical being directly. There is no other type of cognition going on, aside from the fact that the cosmos is working to gestate an ether body. The sensations which the

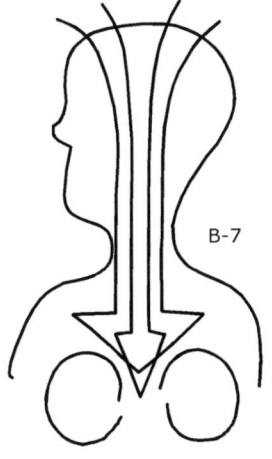

musical and sculptural forces co-operate

children experience are nutrition for their life organs directly.

Now, in the diagram here, I have tried to show a child from birth to seven, and Rudolf Steiner, in *Balance in Teaching*, gives a very interesting picture. He says that the head principle is the area where there is a receiving of these cosmic life forces. It is because the head is really where the gateway to the senses is most concentrated. Through hearing and seeing, mainly, there is an influx, a constant influx, of these cosmic ether forces under the activity of the Ego that is united with them. A part of the cosmic Ego is building the ego organization, which is what will eventually be the instrument and life forces of the partially incarnated cosmic Ego. The ego organization is being built by this cosmic Ego, or true self, by uniting itself with part of the etheric formative forces and bringing them into contact with the physical. There is a kind of drawing down that the true self does; it focuses the ether forces down into the physical. As that happens, the activity is primarily focused in the head region. So the birth-to-seven child has a very large head because that, as we could say in

a kind of funny way, is its antenna, because the antenna is resonant to the signal, and the signal is from the cosmos. This is what enables the child to draw in cosmic forces through the gates of the senses. They are focalized in the head, an image of the cosmos which looks like this.

The cosmic forces come in to the head and they pour out of the head and down into the rest of the body. They are not there in the way they are in the older child, because in the young child the Ego has only partially incarnated into the etheric forces. The etheric forces are not yet freed because the ether body has not yet been born. But they are there working to make the life organs and to complete their forming. So the picture is this: the cosmos working in through the senses from the periphery, then going down and forming liver, lung, kidney, and heart. But the liver, lung, kidney, and heart are being formed in a very cosmic way. Hidden in the music and in the speech, and in what is seen in the environment of the child are forces that are building, forming, structuring. Along with that, those etheric forces that come in contact with the earthly forces are also destroying and decaying, because the ether body, as we have said, is plant-like. The plant grows and decays; that is what it does.

Now we come to one of the difficult parts in *Balance in Teaching,* when Rudolf Steiner gives the picture that the astral body, through the musical forces, creates the processes that he calls upbuilding. In other places, he will say that the astral body is the source of illness, which can seem contradictory. But we have to be very precise as we use these terms, because they are really not contradictory at all. These concepts just require saying beforehand: This is what I am talking about at this particular stage.

In the birth-to-seven child, the ether body—the gestating ether body—dominates. The physical body is built according to that gestation pattern, but there is a kind of turbulence in the gestation. It is just like the experience of you women who have given birth; you know that there is a bit of turbulence that comes into your life during that period. It is the same in the birth-to-seven child. There is a certain turbulence in the body that is being gestated—we could say etheric turbulence. That etheric turbulence manifests itself in the oscillation between *Yes, I am like an angel* and *Now I am less like an angel* that goes on between birth and seven. Sometimes overnight. Sometimes day to day. Sometimes hour to hour. The oscillation moves back and forth between the more dynamic cosmic forces and some very incarnated fixed habit patterns. This is because the ether body, when it falls to earth and becomes earthly, is the source of habit. When these patterns later become free, at the birth of the etheric, they will be the source of temperament. The temperament, then, becomes a problem for the Ego, because the ether forces in it are fixed through habit and may not still have access to the cosmic patterns that are needed to maintain the organism. When we want to change a habit, it is very difficult to do that because the ether body, very early, is formed by particular patterns of sensation. The earthly forces that are given to this young being in the sensations in the environment form patterns in the life organs, which go on and later become temperamental disposition.

There is a picture of this that I have found to be very useful. That is the difference between a suspension and a solution. If we try to understand the activity of the etheric formative forces, we can think in terms of what a suspension is. In a suspension, there is matter suspended in a fluid medium. No matter how fine the matter becomes—we can pulverize it and pulverize it and pulverize it—if we let that sit for a while, the matter will eventually fall out of suspension and become a precipitate at the bottom of the vessel. This is the oscillation between form and decay. When a being is coming into manifestation, it uses the peripheral forces as a kind of forming blueprint or template. Those form-forces are pure life and have not yet attracted matter. That is the role of water. But then, through continued forming and the action of the Ego focused on a relative center, matter is drawn in and gets formed into substance. Once matter gets formed, it comes under the laws of the earth. Then it starts to build and open up, and then comes the law of minimal surfaces and the inevitable disruption of the membrane at the periphery, and then comes the breaking down of the systems. The system that has been formed breaks down into smaller and smaller and smaller pieces. That is decay. Then the pieces go back to earth. In the language of alchemy that is called a salt process. The salt goes into apparent solution and is lifted into a levity state by the water and then the water goes away and the salt comes back out again just as it went in. Chemically, that is a suspension. In a true solution, the salt would never come back out of the liquid. The salt never falling again would be the activity of musical forces. That is what Rudolf Steiner calls upbuilding. That is what we could call cooking. In order to do that, matter has to be taken to a higher and higher level of levity. Tomorrow we'll take a look at that one.

I wanted to bring those two images because they are useful when we try to imagine the disposition of a child, the mood of a child, from birth to seven. As educators, what could we really look for? Even though there is not a temperamental response yet because the temperaments have not actually formed, there is the beginning of a temperamental response in the forming of a particular organ in the preschooler. This first temperamental blush is given by the organ in the body that looks after life. That is the liver.

The liver is connected most directly to the ether forces of forming and decaying, of coming into being and then going away. That is the life of the liver. In the fetus, the liver and the thymus are by far the most dominant metabolic organs in the body for the whole pre-natal development. If you look in the biological evolution of the lower kingdoms for an animal which is mostly liver, you have to go through a lot of phyla until you get up to the crustaceans. The first animal in which the whole body cavity is almost completely filled with a liver is a crayfish. The characteristic life gesture of the crayfish is: Now I'm growing; now I'm hiding. It grows and it grows and it grows, and it gets so big that the law of minimal surfaces takes over. The skin has to split. The skin splits and this very succulent little being comes out of the split skin and finds a hole to crawl into, until it can form another shell so that it is not so tasty. So there is a growth side, a developmental side, and then a kind of an "I'm shutting down and going in to my little hole" side. This is the liver rhythm. It comes from the liver as a kind of picture of the sun, even though the liver is related to Jupiter. The sun rhythm is day and night, and day and night, and day and night. This is decaying—growing: decaying (day)—growing (night).

What we could call the liver mood, or even the crayfish mood, is the source of the mood oscillations of these young ones. They are sweet and lovely and delicate and gentle, and then they turn around and whack their baby brother in the head with their doll. And you wonder: How can this be? When the liver dominates the consciousness, there is tremendous growth, and then a complete shutting down and going within, and resting and covering one's head. We could even say depression. If these forces are not met and harmonized from birth to seven, if there is not a daily rhythm, then the liver, in adulthood, will be trying to return to a stage of development where it can find in its environment forces which allow it to approach its cosmic archetype. It will be searching for rhythmic forces in its environment that allow it to once again get in contact with its life. Unless this is developed and nurtured in the environment of the child from birth to seven, then the liver mood will permeate the rest of the temperamental development in the lower school, and then really erupt in the high school, and then become depression in intellectual soul times.

This is the root of depression. Depression really is a kind of hunger for rhythmic sensation, for sensation which is non-threatening and which can be assimilated or, we could even say, digested into life. As educators, we need to be careful that strong sensation doesn't come so quickly that the children can't digest it. Sensation should also not move abstractly into concepts for the young child, for as soon as young children are challenged with abstract ideas, there is kind of shell that forms around their life forces. Even in adults that happens. So the pictures, and the movements, and the sounds in the environment of the child from birth to seven need to be rhythmically presented with a very keen perception of day to night, and a very keen perception of season to season, because it is that kind of etheric rhythmic force that the liver is listening to as a kind of cosmic digestion of sensation.

Rudolf Steiner gives a picture that the liver is an organ that is an arrested head formation. He gives that in the physiology lectures. When you first read that you say: Whoa, what does that mean? But if we look at the picture that I presented earlier of the head receiving cosmic forces through sensation, and now we look at the liver and the place of the liver in biology, the liver comes out in the embryo as a bud of the digestive system and then lives in the digestion, receiving impulses from the world through the digested food that comes out of the intestines and the lymph. It is, we could say, listening to the sensations of the world in those fluids. The liver sits amid all of that lymph with all of these foodstuffs, and gathers it in. Into that sea of lymph there are tremendous sensations that are playing up through the lymph fluids based on the patterns of sensation in the sympathetic nervous system in the child. Rudolf Steiner connects the sympathetic nervous system to the etheric body, and it is in that ether body that shocks to the system are registered. The sympathetic nervous system brings balance back into a system that has been overloaded or stressed or shocked. So the sympathetic nervous system, especially in the metabolic system, is connected to the movements of the limbs. It reacts to jerking movements in sensations, abruptness, hardness, coarseness; these all register in the physiology of the child, especially in the metabolic organs, as a kind of etheric disturbance. The metabolic system then has to secrete into the lymph all kinds of reactive secretions which cause the liver to say: What's that? What's that? What's that?? Is this okay? Is this all right? Something's going wrong!

The liver, we could say, becomes harried. It is constantly thinking that something is wrong. What it should be thinking is: I wonder what is happening on Jupiter today? That is what the liver is expecting. If it doesn't get Jupiter, if it gets simply that the adrenals and the sympathetic nervous system are dumping secretions that are a stimulus and response to environmental stress, then the liver incorporates that stress in the forming of the proteins, because the liver is a life-formative etheric organ. Because it is an etheric organ, it is a sculptural organ. What it is sculpting is the proteins that will later become liver, lung, kidney, and heart, etc. It does so by listening to the cosmic music and then sculpting the substances that come to it into usable forms for that particular physiology. So, in a way, it is like an arrested head. What it is listening to is the music of the spheres. It uses that music to create little images of Jupiter (liver), and Saturn (bones), and Venus (kidney) in the body. So in *Balance in Teaching* and in various other places, Rudolf Steiner speaks of the liver as a characteristic organ that really needs to be thought about by the kindergarten teacher. The whole physiology and the whole inner life of soul that the child from birth to seven is bringing to Earth is based on an inner clairvoyance as to what is going on in the secretions in the fluids in the body.

The Ego moves in towards the incarnating child. In their inner life children begin having memories of living among the stars. The environment impacts the senses. The children are dimly aware but not consciously aware of how the environmental sensations come into and are reflected by the physical body. The environmental sensations bounce back up because the ether body is very flexible and fluid. They bounce back up into the cosmic astral. The music of the spheres and the cosmic astral says, "I don't know what this is; you take it!" and reflects the personalized environmental sense patterns back down to the etheric, and suddenly the ether body is caught in an oscillation between the cosmic astral and the physical body. The ether body doesn't know what to do with the personalized forces. So what it does is make a little moving model of this oscillating movement. This model is then called adrenaline, or testosterone, or thyroid secretion, or digestive juices. Bodily secretions are a kind of fixed movement model of the stimulus-response pattern—one part per million of adrenaline in the blood coming out of the kidneys, and instantly the whole body is on a fight-or-flight pattern for fifteen minutes. The secretion is an individualized movement. It is a substance that is a concentrated cosmic movement. The child from birth to seven is acting out the patterns of its secretions. That is what Rudolf Steiner is saying. The environment impacts the organs. The life organ tries to accommodate the personalized sensation, but because the way it best does that is by creating secretion, an image of a creative movement, the secretion as movement image then goes into the blood. The child then listens to its own incarnating process through the ether body. It is a child of the cosmos from birth to seven and it acts out what the pattern of stimulus-response would be in the particular organ that is secreting. That, in the language of anthroposophy and in pedagogy, is called fantasy.

The fantasy life of the child is driven by the sensations that are impacting the ether body, this earthly ether body that is creating secretions as images out of the cosmic formative patterns. So if there is acting out, the teacher looks to the environment and tries to create—especially for the liver—a kind of rhythmical massage of the liver. Day after day after day after day, things are presented and then moved on just a little bit, and then just a little bit, and then just a little bit, always building in a rhythmical way, and allowing for very clear pictures to go into sleep. The clearer the picture, the more the liver can get it. The liver has a very dull consciousness. It is not tremendously aware of itself, we could say. It is very much aware of what is coming to it. As a result, you can remove three quarters of your liver and it will regenerate. That is tremendous life. The characteristic of life is that it grows and decays, but it is not terribly aware. So during the birth-to-seven time, there is tremendous life pouring in through the senses of the young child. Fantasy arises in the child as a response to these sensations. The educator who looks at the environment and the rhythm of sensation has the best handle on being able to heal those liver rhythms of waking and sleeping and dreaming—day to day to day.

When that happens in the environment of the children, there will not be a hunger for images when they are thirty-five. They won't succumb to the great temptation of striving to out-do the next person by inundating themselves with sensations. The great struggle of adults today is to somehow transform their sensing so that they become aware that they are citizens of the cosmos as well as citizens of the earth.

The Child from Seven to Fourteen

Lecture given February 22, 2000

One of the most challenging tasks of the Waldorf teacher is in the realm of imagination. Imagination, in the language of Rudolf Steiner, is very different from fantasy. When we looked at the forces in the young child—the etheric embryo of forces that is around the child—in the sheath we saw a picture of the biology and the soul movements of the child as fairly synchronous. They were linked to each other; what was happening in the cosmos was actually becoming flesh. We saw that the forces and the forms that were present as cosmic forces actually made their way directly in, through the embryo, to the physical body of the child. Then from birth to seven, those cosmic forces continued pouring into the child through what could be called a soul placenta, a sheath of forces of the Ego, the cosmic astral, and the cosmic etheric.

After the change of teeth, these forces are still present around the young child, giving it information in the form of sense impressions and gestures and moods that live in the space around it. Rudolf Steiner calls these forces the cosmic nutrition stream. The purpose of that stream is to form images in the child, or we could say fields of activity, which move in a particular way—in what Rudolf Steiner calls a lawful way—to create organs that have as their function the production of living pictures of the way in which the organ came into being out of the cosmos. So we have a lung that has a function in an organism; Rudolf Steiner would describe the forces in the lung as hierarchical forces that eventually came into the form of the lung. Once the lung was formed as an organ, the forces that formed it became the function of the organ. This is known as the esoteric law of organ formation.

This is a very significant picture for the work of the Waldorf teacher, because the content of your lessons in the lower school is still helping to form the physical and etheric organs, even though the ether body has been born. There are living pictures that are present around the young child in nature. In these living pictures, there are certain fields of forces that they have access to even when their ether forces are released at the change of teeth. It is those living pictures, out of the lessons that the teacher gives, that provide a kind of link for the children to the place where they just came from in the cosmos. They provide a link to a world where things work well, where if there is a conflict it is of mythic proportions, where there isn't just smallness and trickery—except for an occasional Loki figure. Outside of trickery, there is what Rudolf Steiner calls the lawful cosmos. Loki is really the potential human being. That lawful cosmos is the realm of the cosmic etheric. The task of the teacher is to somehow wade into the immense mountains of data available on everything from botany to electrical circuits, things that the Waldorf teachers have to somehow grasp in their career as lower school teachers, and somehow, out of all of that very diverse and very technical information, make, for children, pictures that live. It is really an immense task.

It is out of the immensity of that task that the critics who are now denouncing Waldorf, especially in the sciences, are finding the place where they put their crowbar to find an entry into the weak points. The sciences in the Waldorf school are one of its weakest points. The reason is that the sciences require the teacher to have so much expertise in all given subjects in order to be able to form an effective living picture. It is really immense to become specialized enough to grasp a subject well enough that you can distill out from all of the data available just those pictures that make sense to the soul of a child. It is a very daunting task.

I would suggest that you use an alchemical technique rather than the technique you may have learned at university, which is: study, study, study, study, when you don't know something, and keep studying just the facts and you hope one day you'll get the picture. That is university method. The other way is to start out with the picture, and to rhythmically bring the picture to the data in hopes of forming a *living* picture. The living picture is a kind of filter.

One of the great and archetypal living pictures is: something is in the center, and something is on the outside, and they wish to speak to each other. That is the first picture that we started with. That picture of the breathing from the center to the periphery and the periphery to the center is like a filter that can be taken into any realm, any specialized subject, and applied to the data of the specialized subject. Out of the hard data a picture will start to arise of relationships. It is the *relationships* that the child is wanting, not the data. They won't want the data until they get into high school, and then the high school teacher had better have the data! But in the lower school, and in the middle school, the data are less essential than an accurate, living picture.

The question is: How do we know whether the picture we are giving is accurate or living? I would like to suggest to you that the litmus test for an accurate living picture is: Does my picture move (live) in a process in the same way as the phenomenon does? If I can form a picture of a process going through changes—one thing changes into another, changes into another, changes into another—if I can see the links of the changing and reconstruct them accurately in my inner eye, then I can read a book about the data, and I will have a feeling whether or not my soul picture is moving (living) the way in which the data is moving. Goethe called it *higher beholding*. This is a technique which I would suggest to you. Just ask some of the veteran teachers out there and they will tell you that this works, because there is no way that you can have the forces to wade into the technical avalanche of data in specialized subjects—and by this I mean mostly the sciences, or history—without having some form of accurate, living picture. What I'd like to do today, is to take a look at some living pictures that are found in Rudolf Steiner's *Balance in Teaching*.

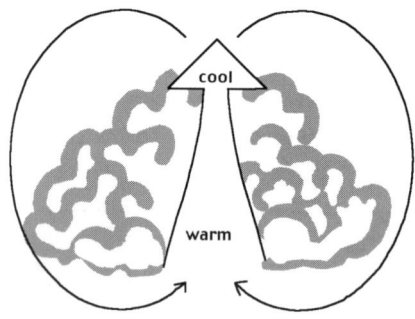

This is a picture of a cloud. Coming up out of the cloud there is an arrow going up. It goes up and then two arrows turn down. Below the cloud there are two arrows turning and going up under the cloud. What this picture represents is a convection cell. The cloud that we see in the sky is the corpse of invisible supersensible activity, a dialogue between warmth and cold that surrounds every cloud in a whole field of organized movement. Underneath every cloud, every cumulus cloud especially, there is warm air rising in a column. So when you look up at cumulus clouds in the sky, underneath every one of those clouds is a rising column of warm air. This is well known to seagulls. They really understand this because their whole body is tuned to differences in temperature and pressure in the air.

That warm column of air may have had a birthing out in some mega mall on the parking lot, and then started to string out as warm air rose, and then pulled off of the parking lot and drifted until we saw it at its upper end giving birth to a cloud. Once the cloud actually forms, that is a picture of the movement of the warm air that has had to lose some of the moisture that it carried up. The technical term for this is condensation. It is a kind of a consolidation of the warmth and moisture in the cloud. It forms, we could say, a little organ, a little sky organ—a cloud. That little sky organ, in its condensing, releases some of the warmth that had carried the water up. The warm water vapor gets up to a certain height and gets so cold that it can't hold on to the warmth any more. The colder the vapor gets, the denser it gets. So, in the surrounding cold air, the warmth being released by the condensing vapor goes up in the cloud. The cooled vapor condenses and falls out as droplets. The water appears as moisture droplets moving down, and the warm air rises rapidly above the cloud. It is then an updraft. But as the warm air rises rapidly, it has lost its moisture and so the warm air cools very rapidly through evaporation. As it cools it starts to sink, so on the outside of every cumulus cloud, there are currents of very cold air going back down. The law is that, when air goes down and compresses, it starts to warm. So as the cold air goes down and compresses into the layer below the condensation layer, it gets warmer. Suddenly it is in a warm and moist environment where it picks up moisture, turns around, and goes right back up again. Every cloud is a rolling doughnut of warm and cold forces. The cloud, as an organ, is a picture of the forces that are around it.

This is a very clear picture in nature of the conditions Rudolf Steiner has described as existing on Old Saturn. It is the picture of the forming of an organ. There are supersensible forces around the organ, which give rise to its form. Once the organ is formed, the forces become the function of the organ. The cloud is sustained by the convection cell of the interchange of the warmth and the cold. It goes through its life as a little sky organ for maybe thirty minutes, unless it finds a big pool of warm air below it, and then it suddenly moves up a notch and becomes larger. If it finds some cold air below it, it starts to shut down and the organ goes away, because the conditions of its genesis are no longer present.

I give this to you as a picture of what we considered on the first day between the Kyriotetes and the Spirits of Motion and the Thrones. It is a kind of a dialoguing and breathing between the periphery and the center, but seen as a lawful, living picture in nature. The warmth rises in the center, the cold descends from the periphery. It is the same picture, but now we have it in the forming of what we could call an organ. The organ is formed by the forces around it that are supersensible, and once the organ is formed, the forces have become the function of the organ.

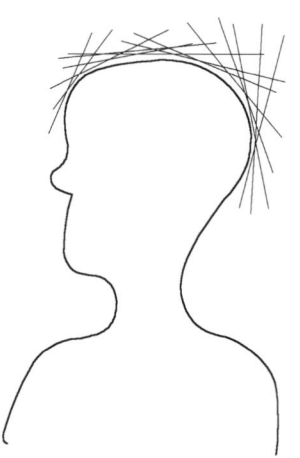

On the opposite page is a diagram of the arrangements that I described yesterday in the life body and the sheath of the child from birth to seven. The figure shows the outline of the child; above we have ether forces that have been caught by the Ego and brought down into a form and incarnation. Rudolf Steiner, in the later parts of *Balance in Teaching,* calls those forces sculptural. If you read between the lines in *Balance in Teaching,* you will see that he is really describing as sculptural forces what in other places, notably *Anthroposophy, a Fragment,* he refers to as the sense of the idea.

Rudolf Steiner, in very early works calls the sense of idea *visualization.* He later drops that because it got confused with vision, but in the earlier works he says that visualization has nothing to do with vision per se, and everything to do with the processes surrounding form. It has everything to do with the ability to inwardly picture a form, especially the form of an idea—the "becoming" of an idea. This is because an idea is really an organ in the soul. It is like a cell in the soul. So what a cell is to the physical body, a concept is to the soul. A concept is like a little cell. Then we take one concept and another concept and another concept to make a tissue of concepts. Then finally if we have enough of these tissues of concepts, we have a living concept.

The life forces, the etheric forming forces, have as a potential the ability to form. They are what an alchemist would call salt forces. They come from nothing into something and then go back again into nothing. Every time they come back, they come back into the same form as the one in which they went out. If you took some salt and put it in water and warmed it and it went out of our perception but then came back as salt after evaporation, you would think that is fine. If it came back as sugar, you would be surprised. In a salt situation, we expect that what goes away should come back as it was before.

That is what we expect with our ideas. We file them away. It is like wondering: Where are my keys? and we expect that they will be in the same place when we go to look for them the next day. The older you get, sometimes that expectation is not an option. We would say that it is because you don't have enough salt available in your thinking. You have it in other places, usually in your joints!

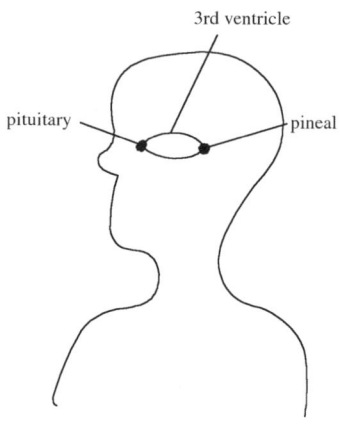

That process of something going into a more rarified state and then coming back again is the analog of the sculptural forces. If you read carefully in *Balance in Teaching*, Rudolf Steiner gives the picture that these forces come from within the human being, within the head. That is where he places them, within the head. They are the forces of what will later be thinking or ideation. But in the young child they are not yet thinking; they are, we could say, the thinking of the cosmos. The cosmos thinks and organs are built. These are the etheric formative forces. In the diagram those forces are in the head inside the form which resembles a little mouth shape. This is in Rudolf Steiner's work in other places. He says that between the pituitary and the pineal glands the little mouth shape there is a field of activity where the two beat into each other, and that is where day consciousness arises. This is in the third ventricle of the brain. I have a sneaking suspicion that, in that area, that is specifically where the forces of form pour into us. In the ancient language, that area was called the womb of the immaculate conception. In anatomy it is the third ventricle. It is a place where new forms come into being—thinking in pictures.

Now in the young child, these sculptural forces come into being, but they impact the child directly in forming the liver or the lung or the kidney. There is no freedom in the child in this forming. If the child says, "I don't want to use those liver forces to do that," it makes no difference; the liver forces simply are what comes. That is one stream, the sculptural stream. But in *Balance in Teaching,* Rudolf Steiner says that the form stream, or that sculptural stream, is woven through and cooperates with another stream that he calls the musical stream. This is music-speech. If you also look at the way he describes music or the sense of the word early on, he says the sense of the word is not the content of the meaning of the word, but is the *tone* of the word, the soul-tone.

Let's paint a picture. Someone comes in and says, "Your car has rolled into the center of the parking lot and there's a tow truck with a policeman standing by it." You could say, "Oh?" (casual), or you could say, "Oooooh" (interested), or "OOOH!" (excited). It is the same word but a different soul tone. The word as tone has different tonal pseudopods of meaning that go out and touch different aspects or life-gestures in the soul. This is what actors do all the time. They play with things like this. This is the word sense.

When Rudolf Steiner first described the senses, he only described nine of them. He characterizes this word sense as a kind of tonal hearing of word-moods. In *Balance in Teaching*, he uses the same shading when he refers to speech and to music. He describes speech and music as if he were describing tone. This is in contrast to the idea of the word. Music/speech is more like a hearing into the tone of the word. Rudolf Steiner said that that was really the *sense* of word. When we cognize the meaning of the word, we are no longer in a sensation. We lift it away from the sensation of the sound profile, or the sound gestalt, of the word—the tonal gestalt of the word—into what we think it means as an abstract idea.

I don't think, in my reading of *Balance in Teaching*, that Rudolf Steiner, in saying music/speech, is talking about making definitions of words. He is really speaking about what he calls the Dionysian principle, the artistic principle. It is that artistic principle that is woven into the current of sculptural form in the early life of the child from birth to seven that gives rise to the Dionysian flexibility within the organs which enables them to listen to each other. This must be in the organism so that the heart can listen to the liver and the liver can listen to the kidney, etcetera. If it was only etheric form, it wouldn't be able to listen. There is a weaving of the two, sculpture and music, from birth to seven that creates the organ and its processes.

Yesterday we said the organ that really dominates the soul life of the preschool child is the liver because that is what is receiving most of the life. But now let's shift to the child who has had a physical birth, then goes through a period of development, and then approaches the change of teeth. In the pre-adolescent phase from seven to fourteen, the pre-etheric forces that were in the cosmos get locked by the ego into a pattern of form and incarnation, and the organs are formed—just as our cloud was formed. But if that was all there was to our evolution, the forming of the organs, then we would have a physical body and an etheric body, but there would be very little left for the soul. All would unfold according to the cosmic plan of the hierarchies. Rudolf Steiner is very careful to say that the cosmic forces do not include per se, the qualities of the soul.

The cosmic forces are what we could call *the given*; they are the created cosmos. They are the sense world, and if they are the sculptural forces, they are the world of the correctness of the concept. The soul is neither the sense world nor the concept. It is something that arises in between as a kind of a who-knows-what-this-is mood among the creative Hierarchies. What is this thing, this soul? How is it that these beings on this planet have been allowed to have this? Look at what they are doing with it? Can we do something about this?

As answer, what we can all do, as I understand it, is to watch, because no one really knows what this thing called soul could be. The book hasn't been written yet. We are writing it even as we speak, and that is the challenge that breaks in upon this paradisical consciousness of the child from birth to seven. Something happens.

According to Rudolf Steiner, these etheric formative forces are powerful in their cosmic form-creating inertia. If they were all we had, we would simply be plants. For humans who are maturing, the hierarchies take those etheric-driven formative forces and pull them back. They pull them back just a little bit.

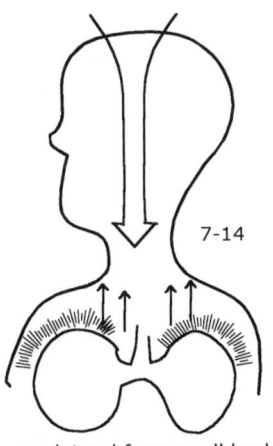

7-14

That's the shorter arrow from above. Now when these etheric forces are held back, these organs (the liver, lung, kidney, and heart) are not being impressed so much from the outside by this cosmic force that is known in the regular

sculptural forces pull back as free forces rise off of the internal organs world as the biological imperative. The soul denies the biological imperative.

Actually, the soul denies a lot of powerful imperatives such as gravity and things like that. The soul says, "I don't want to adhere to the law of gravity; I have things to do and places to go. So gravity, you wait a while. I'll come under the spell of gravity mostly at night, because during the day I've got things to do." Every one of you is defying the law of gravity in the most mysterious way possible right at this moment.

So in the maturing human being, the biological imperative, the cosmic given, pulls back. As it pulls back, the organs, which were being formed in lawful ways, suddenly find that around them there is a little atmosphere, a little play of forces. The organs have been, in the words of Rudolf Steiner, "consolidated." The child has reached a certain stage of development where it says, "Thank you very much," to the cosmic formative forces. "I now have a complete set of organs, and I'll prove it. I'll take even the hardest parts of the stuff that's left over from the old cosmos, my teeth, and I'll throw them out. I'll put them under my pillow so maybe the fairies can come and talk to me again for old time's sake. I don't need these anymore because I have something else I want to do. Thank you, Father God, for providing these milk teeth for me, but I'm going to take them and I'm going to give them back to the fairies."

When that happens, the inner life of the child begins to enter into a space that has never really been there before for that being. That is the space around the organ from which the supersensible forces that used to be driving in from the cosmos have now pulled back. There is a free space around the organ where the consciousness of the soul can enter in. The individuality says, "Oooh! **I AM**." Not quite so consciously, but it begins to have the experience of what it would be like, for instance, to have a secret. "Oh, if I just hold this secret in that little free space in myself, I can look mommy right in the eye and say, 'He did it!' and she won't be able to tell."

That's very interesting, because that ability allows me to have a whole inner life that has nothing to do with anyone else except ME. That's what we call a free space. The child between seven and fourteen is extremely aware of what is going on in the free space of ME. That's why it is always testing. Do you have any authority over ME or is this free? Can I do what I want or do you have the last say?

Children want to sense that the beings who are around them are also in contact with free space. That's the love part of the authority. According to Rudolf Steiner, the two great forces of teaching are authority and love. The love part—on the part of the teacher—is: "Yes, I can understand. As a being who lives in my own free spaces (at certain times during the day), I can understand your free spaces." The children can understand your free spaces because that is where you both meet at night.

In that area around the organ of the pre-adolescent, there is a little battle going on. It is not quite yet a pitched battle. Pre-adolescents know where the keys are, but they are still afraid to get into the car. They know where mommy keeps the keys. She keeps them under her pillow with all the teeth for the fairies, right? So, they know where all that is, but they still haven't quite gotten the courage to steal the key. They haven't taken the key in their hand, which they will have to do in order to become an I-being. But here, in the pre-adolescent, we see the very first glimmerings of that.

Each organ that has been formed has around it a little sheath of free forces. The pre-adolescent child makes a game out of looking around at beings and saying, "Hmm, my teacher seems to get a lot of free forces from her liver. I'll try testing that for a while." Then they try what it would be like to be liver-focussed for a while. Then they say, "Oh, I did that once last year; it's kind of boring. Now there's this cute little girl and she bounces all over the place. I think I'm going to try some kidney sheath forces for these next couple weeks; maybe she'll talk to me if I do that." So then they take on kidney forces. "Well that's not really me, but it was kind of fun while it lasted, wasn't it?"

This experimenting with organ forces is what we call temperament. They are getting access to a particular type of force field that moves in a particular way, but now it has been freed up so that they can have in their inner life an experience of, "Yes, I can put on a sanguine temperament and take it off like a coat." That's also free. They can look at people around them and say, "How is it that it has become this way with you?" as sort of a pre-Parzival consciousness. Then they look at their parents: "Boy I wonder how it got this way with them? I don't know. I think maybe I was a changeling. I'm pretty sure, because I definitely wouldn't have picked these two; just look at the way this is going on here."

Holding things at arm's length is what is possible when we have free forces around an organ, because around the organ are imaginations that used to be a part of the forming process of the organ. Now they are not a part of the forming of the organ. There is a part of them where the pressure to be a particular form is somewhat lessened from the side of the cosmos, and the pictures of the forming process now rise up towards the head as what Rudolf Steiner calls imaginations. They are the formative imaginations of the organ, but now a little portion of them is free. They rise up and they become inner pictures that the child can control, instead of receiving a picture from the outside, as happens from birth to seven, when a child may have a stick and then suddenly somebody says spaceship, and suddenly it turns into a spaceship. Or somebody says gun, and mommy says no gun, and so the child says: Uhhh, okay, doll!

To the preschooler in fantasy consciousness, the stick can be anything, because the stimulus is coming from the outside, but after and during the change of teeth, the stimulus is coming from the inside. There is a space inside where the picture can be mulled over and edited according to the needs of the soul. The child contains information which can be given, and the child can hold back information. Certain people can be accepted in and certain people can be held away.

It's that repertoire of temperamental dispositions, of sympathies and antipathies, that the child begins to become extremely aware of. This comes out of the free forces rising off of the life organs. They are free imaginations that are rising up. In the ancient world, this was the basis of clairvoyance. Rudolf Steiner calls it belly clairvoyance. The images arise from the inside; they flood the soul with a certain kind of cosmic content from the hierarchies, and then the oracle speaks. The children then are experiencing a kind of recapitulation of the mystery wisdom of these imaginations, very clear imaginations, that you folks are giving them through your lessons in mythology.

Joseph Campbell says a myth is an argument between two organs in the body. Rudolf Steiner tells the physicians, in the medical lectures, that if you want to study physiology, study mythos. Don't go to *Gray's Anatomy*; or, rather, go to *Gray's Anatomy*, but with a living picture. Go to *Gray's Anatomy* and look for Zeus, then you are doing something. He says, especially in the anatomy of the brain, go to mythos. In the myths you will find analog pictures—living, imaginative pictures of the way in which the physical organs are interacting. That is the power of myth. So your lessons in myth, whether you know it or not, are giving you the basis of your physiology block, and are setting the stage for all that is going to happen in the high school through analysis science. The basis of that accuracy is the degree of soul lawfulness through which you can live into the dialogue in the myth. The soul yearns for living pictures, artistically presented.

We come, then, to the function of the musical forces. If the formative forces, the conceptual forces, pull back a little bit, what happens is that the musical forces have a little more play around the organ. These musical forces live in questions like: What is the tone of what you are saying? What is the tone of just the way you are carrying yourself? What is the tone of the way you stand in front of me and you move?

What is that tone? Children between seven and fourteen are very aware of it. They live in that tone. That is why Rudolf Steiner says they are naturally artistic. To them everything has a feeling tone which is more important than the concept of the thing. Every color, every shape, every person, everything they eat, has a feeling tone—the sky, nature, everything. It's a palette of feeling, but the feelings are not personal feeling per se. That comes later, in high school. They are still living in a little cloud of paradise that allows them to say: This person has this kind of tone and that person has that kind of tone. They can't bring the awareness to day-waking consciousness, but they know exactly what it is, because they can just meet and match it.

You have probably noticed that in your class. You come in on Monday. You have had something that happened in your life that you are supposed to leave at the door—but you know how it is—so it comes in the classroom with you, and that is what you hear coming back to you from the children.

Why? Because they are just picking that up from your tone and they seek to become that. They don't want to *imitate* it; they feel drawn to *becoming* it. If they were little children, they would imitate your tone. That's the danger of teaching kindergarten. The older children don't want to imitate your tone; they want to observe it and say: How is it that it has become like this with you, teacher?

The freeing up of these soul forces allows the musical forces to be present unconsciously. The artistic element in the soul is watching the tone of the formative forces coming in. The unconscious artist asks: Just how is the liver doing this; just how is the kidney doing this? The unconscious artist does not do it consciously; it is done subconsciously, but it is done none the less. Physiologically, the organ that is a picture of this unconscious tonal sensing is the lung.

The biography of the lung is that it starts out as a bud on the intestines. It is a metabolic, digestive organ. It is closed off, and it feels very comfortable being so. Then, slowly, through the first nine months, the lung makes its way up the digestive tract, up across the diaphragm. As soon as it gets up across the diaphragm, a force from the mouth starts to move in from the outside of the embryo. A cosmic force moves in and pushes a tube down towards the lung. The two travel towards each other until suddenly the lung reaches the bucal fold, and there is an opening. Then suddenly this hidden inward digestive organ is now forced to open up and deal with the whole sense world. Ouch.

This is the source of much of the soreness of the soul of the years seven to fourteen. Here we have little beings that in a short span of time have come from the womb, into contact with mom and dad, then maybe spent some time in daycare or kindergarten, and now are thrust into first grade with its lessons, pencils, homework, etcetera. There is a mood of, "I feel like I am on an express train going towards something that I have no idea what it is and I'm not sure I want to do this. I was really happy playing in the mud back there in kindergarten." That new mood, we could say, is the impact of the great wounding.

The lung is afraid of being on earth, because what the lung has to do is take all of the carbon from all of the things that we eat and dump it overboard, or else the physical body becomes like a board. The lung has a fear. It is afraid of responsibility, of having to own up to things, having to get tons of data and digest that. Data is death to the lung. The lung gets data as just dust. The lung wants to go in an out and in and out and in and out, and yet the lung is one of the most consolidated, sclerotic organs of the body. The liver is 96 percent fluid, and the lung is bound in cartilage. It is a miracle that we even breathe. It is a miracle of pneumatic engineering, because the lung is not a floppy little bag; it is really a hard, crusty organ. In the words of Rudolf Steiner, it is very consolidated. In its consolidation it is carrying the burden of the soul meeting the world.

In biology, in the evolution of the animal world, you don't find anything even faintly resembling a lung as we know it among the vertebrates until very late, in the mollusks, the highest of the invertebrates. What you will find in a mollusk, in a clam, is that the clam surrounds itself with very sensitive membranes, like placental membranes. What the clam is doing with those membranes is eating and breathing, simultaneously. There is mucous all over the membrane. Fluid from the surrounding water comes in with food particles, and they get stuck in the mucous, and the clam pushes the mucous towards its mouth with little hairs. On our lungs we have cilia just like this for moving debris out of the lung. The clam has that to move mucous into its mouth and that is an image of the human lung.

In the mollusk we have an analog of what will later become the respiratory system in the human being. If we look at the life of the mollusk, we can get a feeling for this mood of the lung that is prevalent in the seven- to fourteen-year-old child. It says, "Don't touch me too hard or I will snap shut. If you leave me alone, I will open my shell in my own way and I will start interacting. But I want to do it on my own terms." The great drama of the mollusk is that over time it becomes encased in its own exhalations. The shell of the mollusk is really solidified breath that has been cast off from this lung. The exhalation meets the seawater and forms a shell. That shell is the emotional shell that the pre-adolescent is experiencing when it opens up and the world comes rushing in.

The Fall that the children go through opens their eyes, and the world starts pouring into a very very tender place. That tender place that the world starts pouring into between the little open parts of the shell, that tender place, is the space of the free forces in the soul. The free forces are the gestating astral body. They are what will later be a fully developed soul capacity, but they are now in gestation. The pre-adolescent is just learning how to enter into them. They are so tender and so open and so new and so free, that impacts from the world must be somehow musical, appropriately musical. The tone of them has to be appropriate. It doesn't matter so much about the data or the concept. Everything matters about the tone, the way in which the pictures, the data, are presented, with living pictures given artistically and rhythmically.

The real key to the astral body is rhythm. The rhythm of the lesson that the lung is really looking for is that there needs to be a balancing. The lung's experience, which is *this is not that* in your lesson—this factuality—needs to be balanced with: "I'm sorry; I know it's creative, but we don't spell that word that way." The lung says, "This is not that." This is the tone of earth gesture. This tone of earth must be experienced to be sure. If it is experienced in a context where "this is *becoming* that," then the teaching can enter into the *process* of how that word is spelled that way, whether through phonetics or clapping or whatever. The curriculum is filled with ways of doing that, of transforming these sculptural and musical forces to keep them oscillating back and forth in the soul.

The real task of the lower school teacher is to somehow introduce to this young child the world, with all its data and all the facts and all the responsibilities and all the scary things, but in a loving, authoritative way using *rhythm* and *process* to balance the giving of the facts. Once the child becomes adept at working in the free space, it becomes rather intoxicated. The free space, when the child moves actually into adolescence, becomes the place where the great battle is to occur. But in pre-adolescence it is not quite a pitched battle yet, although you can certainly see signs of it around nine years old when the cynic comes out in the children. In the children who used to be loving and open, suddenly something happens. That is a sign. That is a barometer saying: Storm warning! There is about to be a big change happening. The key in that middle realm in the lower school is to keep the heart and the lung moving between fact and process and fact and process, in an artistic way so that these free forces and the musical tone forces in the soul can enter into relationships with the facts of the world in creative learning experiences.

The Adolescent from Fourteen to Twenty-one

Lecture given February 23, 2000

Today we'll take a turn towards the wild side a little bit. It is in the high school that the largest challenge against anthroposophy as a dogma is waged. The difference between dogma and anthroposophy—and *true* anthroposophy—is the cultivation of the inner life. If you speak anthroposophy and you are not working on yourself in the inner life, then living anthroposophy becomes a dogma. If you are actually working on yourself as a regular practice, then no matter what it is that you bring out of anthroposophy, it will have the ring of truth. It is the sense of truth that is the challenge for the high school teacher. Authority works very well in the kindergarten because there a natural imitative gesture is living. Authority with love works very well in the lower school, because there is still a kind of lingering of the cloud of glory that is trailing behind the young child. But there is a Rubicon! All ye who enter here abandon hope! That's called being thirteen years old.

As we move into adolescence and the teenage years, there is a tremendous battle in the soul of the young person, and the battle is one-on-one, them against themselves. You may, if you teach them, have the experience that it is them against you, but that is really not the case. They have come from paradise, have set up a little encampment there in their body, have begun to live in it a little bit and understand the controls. They finally are understanding the manual for how to install the software. They can get around a little bit and now, suddenly, the rules completely change. Instead of really trusting the people around them, they trust no one, not even their friends. But they will cling to their friends desperately, in hopes that they can trust them.

There is a fundamental requirement of this age of adolescence, and that is: When I speak to you and you speak to me, can you give me a feeling in my soul that what we are sharing is true? They get this feeling by applying the musical forces of tone to what they hear and what they see. They live in a tonal fabric of emotions, feelings, soul-movements, antipathies, and sympathies that create, in the Wagnerian sense, a kind of great artwork of life. Speech, drama, music, and even mathematics: to the adolescent, all of these are riddled with drama—not so much the drama of the mathematics as a subject, but of who is sitting next to me in second period mathetmatics. That changes their experience of math class very strongly! If it is the right person then maybe they will finally get a B in math instead of a C, because there is an incentive to be there in mathetmatics. The incentive is an emotional one. It is a feeling incentive.

They are adept enough to take the concepts that are given to them by adults, to adopt them and put them on like a coat. They learn that in the lower school through their temperament. Then they model back what is given to them, if they choose to. If the inner meter of feeling says, "Yes this person can be modeled," then you will get back almost exactly what you are giving out. They are very brightly polished mirrors of pathology. So what you give to them is what they give back to you with unerring accuracy. The reason they can do that is that they have just come into a wealth of forces that are totally free. We could say they have just given birth to their astral body.

Their astral body, in the cosmos, is connected to the ability to go against everything else. You can understand this if you look in the work of Elisabeth Vreede. Rudolf Steiner said of Elisabeth Vreede that she was the only person who ever understood everything he said. That's a big deal. After Rudolf Steiner's death, she continued the letters to the members that he was writing at the time of his death—under a certain duress from certain colleagues, I might add, but she continued them. She continued them and formed them in an astronomical way. If I were to title that book now for broader consumption it would be: *Everything You Ever Wanted to Know About Anthroposophy But Were Afraid to Ask.* In the first volume of these astronomical letters she described the movements of the planets as pictures of the deepest mysteries of Rudolf Steiner's work in the context of celestial motion. There she describes the astral plane as the potential for planets to go retrograde. It is through the retrograde motion of planets, the apparent looping of planets, that the organ-forming principle arises in physiology. Planet looping, in that particular realm, provides forces in the field of the embryo that allow it to form loops within its intestines, otherwise known as lung, kidney, and heart. In this view, the fundamental formation of the organ is a result of relative motions between two planets.

Now this is a startling picture that she gives, and she even connects it to the work of the adversaries. It is that forming principle that has somehow come out of the cosmic spaces, through the starry realm, and suddenly becomes something that we could call a very local phenomenon, because in actuality, in celestial mechanics, there is no such thing as a retrograde loop. It is only apparent, as viewed from the Earth, because of the relative motions of planets. If you haven't studied astronomy, this may be difficult to understand, but if you are a Waldorf teacher, you probably will be able to get this picture. That apparent motion, retrograde motion—going against the grain, we could say—is adolescence. It is the feeling that, "I know the whole cosmos is going in one direction, but you know, today I feel like digging in my heels. Why? Don't ask me because I'm really not aware of it, but I know definitely that that is what I am going to do."

In order to deal with this effectively, the high school teacher can say things in a certain tone. For example, when you are right in the middle of the first fifteen minutes of main lesson, and Johnny comes in the back door and slams the door so that everyone turns and does a double take on Johnny, you say, "Thank you Johnny for coming, but I see you brought your attitude with you today. Perhaps you can leave your friend, your attitude, outside; *you* can come in, but *it* must stay outside. You can pick up on it later!!" And Johnny will do a little double take on your weirdness, and will consider options for a moment just for a little dramatic flair, but Johnny will usually deposit the shadow outside and come in, because he is probably burned out anyway, and it is not worth the fight. It started long before he got to your class. You are just getting the previews of the rest of Johnny's day.

That type of mood transforming can be done in that space, because there is a space to do it. Adolescents, if they are spoken to that way, can recognize that there is a difference between copping an attitude and being an attitude. They know that, because that is where they live all the time! If you know that too, then you are somehow in on the great secret. The challenge of the high school teacher is to have a way of saying, "Is this really the soul of the person saying this, or is this something that is reverberating in weird space today—or this week, or this year?" To be able to tell the difference, teachers need to immerse themselves daily in a dialogue with their own retrograde forces. That is what teachers in the high school bring to the children, the work they do on themselves. That is what the children in the high school expect. They expect that, when that teacher comes in, there are some things that have happened. They expect that the teachers have actually *done* what they are talking about. That is a very big deal. If they haven't done what they are talking about, there is an instant radar in the student that says, "Tune this out." That's the first thing. That is what we could call the feeling of the trust that this teacher is a person standing in the world.

It doesn't matter so much to the lower school child how the teacher is standing in the broader world, especially in the first part of the lower school. But as they go through the Fall from Paradise, and as the free forces start to get more free, the astral body starts to invade, like a mushroom invading a host. It starts to permeate the whole soul life, because suddenly there is a free space. There is a crack; there is a spot where something new can go—and flow into the cosmos.

Freedom is initially brought through a kind of subconscious *inability* to be in that free space consciously. It is a weak spot in the soul, the astral body. It is a wound. But the *gift* of the astral body is that it can be incredibly flexible. Flexibility is its problem and that is also its gift. The problem of the etheric body is that it can be a bit stodgy. That is the problem of the etheric body and that is its gift. Your wound is always your strength.

The children in the high school are experimenting with that, *big time!* They wear their wounds as badges of honor. That's why the funny hair; that's why the strange looks and accoutrement. Where they are wounded is what they put out as a badge of honor, and it is not really personal to the adult who is charged with teaching them. Although if you are in front of it day after day, it may get that way. We can all understand that. The real question in high school education is: Can you give me the *feeling* of truth through who you are? I'm looking around me, says the high school student, for people who are participating in a dialogue with truth. They don't even have to have the right answers, as long as they are willing to admit that they don't have the right answers.

That stance is often more important than having all the right answers, because if they want answers, they can just go on the Internet. There you can get plenty of answers. High schoolers all know that the information superhighway is a bogus thing from one perspective because you can get "answers" to anything, and you still have the same problem. Is it true? A high school student may become attracted to the Internet simply by the volume of the answers. The question remains: Is information automatically knowledge?

So the challenge of the high school teacher is to develop an organ of perception in the soul of the student that is the equivalent of a life organ in the body. The difference is that the life organs were created by the cosmos in the lower school child. What we are doing in education during adolescence is creating organs of spiritual perception in the soul. What we are doing in the kindergarten and the first parts of the lower school is finishing the work of the hierarchies that are creating life organs in the body. In the kindergarten, we are helping the child to finish the life organs by providing the proper environment in which they can imitate first and then emulate.

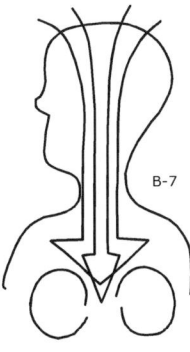
musical and sculptural forces co-operate

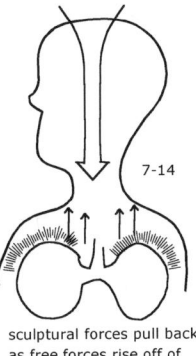
sculptural forces pull back as free forces rise off of the internal organs

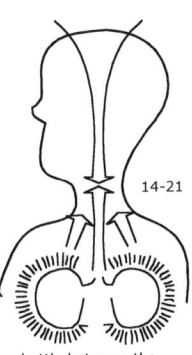
battle between the musical and sculptural forces in the larynx

If we look at the diagrams from birth to seven, the liver is being formed by the cosmos. From seven to fourteen, the lungs dominate the soul life, bringing a kind of sensitivity to the cosmic forces in the play of cooperation between the forming forces of the inner life and the musical forces streaming in from the outside. As educators, the task is to integrate the sense life and the inner life of thinking in rhythmic ways. In the diagram of the adolescent, what we can see is that the arrow that was coming down (the formative forces, the sculptural forces) has receded now, and it gets about as far down in the organism as the larynx. The formative forces are no longer penetrating and creating livers; they are maintaining livers. The creative part of the etheric formative forces is now inside the head, creating little analogs of livers that it puts out and spreads around in the world. These are called depressive moments or something like that. These temperamental moods are little organs that are little models of what a liver would be, but now they are in the emotional life of the soul, like little islands of feelings. *I feel good; I feel terrible*—these are liver imaginations. *This is not that*—lung imaginations.

When the children are finishing off the lung, if something traumatic happens during that time, then the tone of the event goes into the forming of that life organ. The incorporated soul tone becomes a challenge in adulthood. We often need to go back and work through the tone gestalt so that the organ can take in the picture in a clearer way. This becomes the challenge of adult education and even beyond. You have to find out where the tone discomfort was in the biography. This is truly then the Parzival question: What ails thee, uncle? Rudolf Steiner says we have to have a loving interest in the other's pathology. The key there is *loving*.

In this sequence of events, what is happening in the pre-adolescent becomes even more amplified in the adolescent. The formative forces withdraw into the head and no longer permeate the body, because their task has been completed long ago. The etheric formative forces stop at the larynx, because the larynx becomes then a vehicle for the formative force of the word, for idea. The larynx becomes a womb for words.

In the adolescent, a stopping and hovering of the soul around the larynx becomes the ability to form incredibly convoluted abstractions. Adolescents get an idea, and then they just work it, and work it in a cerebral frenzy, and every once in a while a burst of feeling comes from the metabolic organs as a great emotional attachment to this idea. Due to a natural lack of cognitive experience, the idea usually comes out as an abstraction. As soon as it is met with, "Oh, well are you sure?" The usual response is, "THIS IS THE WAY I SEE IT." And, "Mr. Teacher, we both know that my feelings are just as valid to me as your facts are to you." If you teach in the high school you know that one. The rationale is, "Well I really *feel* this, and I don't want to be put down by a lot of facts, you know? Facts are okay if they prove my point, but if they don't prove my point then you have to honor my feelings." That attitude can be a bit of a dilemma in math and science!

The picture of the dynamic here is that the musical forces, coming in from the sense world, have indeed formed the organs of metabolism. By adolescence they have formed and finished them, but they keep pouring into the organs, so much so that around the organs a little cloud of extra free forces starts to grow. When that happens in an organ, the organ gives rise to bursts of forces that are free, that rise up into the consciousness. Rudolf Steiner calls these bursts organ dreams. There is a kind of dreaming that drifts up from below that also gets stuck in the larynx area. It doesn't ever quite get up into the head, except when occasionally it can manage to penetrate through the larynx and get up into the head. It usually arises as pictures of intense desire, because really the substance of these metabolic forces is will.

In the adolescent, there is an ever-increasing tide of will coming up from the metabolic organs, rising and overwhelming the rhythmic system, going up and punching through the larynx where there is a battle. In boys the battle can be seen as their voice changes radically in pitch. That is a real battle. When the voice cracks and is high, it is saying, "I'm going back to the ether forces." When the voice becomes low, it is saying, "Now I'm coming down into the metabolic forces." The cracking of the voice is a cracking through of the metabolic forces rising up and overcoming the original creative forces pouring through the head. This is a battle royal, within the self. What has been the dominant modality, and could be trusted and leaned upon, which was the imaginations coming from the cosmos, is now shut off. Now there is something coming up from below, feelings of immense attraction to people who, seven years ago, would just be good for pulling their pigtails, and throwing mud at. Now suddenly it's, "I wonder what our kids would look like?" That's a big switch!

When that happens in the inner life, it is no wonder that there is turmoil and confusion. It arises as a complete thing. You *can* actually imagine what your children would look like. Why? Because you now have an active belly clairvoyance, and your stock-in-trade is organ dreams. You become an expert at organ dreaming, and some of the organs which you dream about yield some pretty interesting dreams. Those dreams are what we could call the creative forces. They come rising up, and suddenly, sitting in the back of the classroom, you are totally overwhelmed with metabolic creative energy, but you don't really have a place to put it. You are biologically prepared, but emotionally totally unprepared.

What has to happen is that, from this flow coming upwards from below, there needs to be a counterflow from above. One counterflow is the force of cognition. What has happened to the etheric formative forces, the sculptural forces, is that they have been locked in the head. Eventually they have to protect themselves from what is coming up from below by actually having some reasons with which to meet the uprising chaos. But the reasons don't come till later. Right now there is just a kind of awareness that, "My goodness, this really is strong, this force coming up from below, these sensations that are connected to my astral body." So the great mantra of the adolescent is: My sensations are *my* sensations. It starts in the pre-adolescent but becomes an art form in the adolescent. My sensations are *my* sensations— and they are unique to me as a unique individual. And you better check it out, because, if you don't, then you are just one of those fossils who don't understand the world. The adolescent landscape is really made out of feelings. All the rest of this stuff is fine, and I'll do it so I can get into Stanford and get my dad off my back, but, as my teacher, you need to recognize my feelings are *my* feelings.

Now, that's the astral body in the adolescent, but it is what Steiner calls the small astral. The big astral is still Jupiter and Saturn and Venus and Mars and the Sun and the Moon, and it is still there, working and moving. It is still present in the sheaths as the possibility of dreaming really big dreams. That is there in the background, but the overwhelming imagination from the adolescent's metabolic organs creates, not so much an awareness of the meaning of the sensations that are happening, but that my sensations are *my* sensations. In the next phase, the big mantra is: My sensations *mean* something—which is what Rudolf Steiner calls the sentient body. That is the stage from twenty-one to twenty-eight. But from fourteen to twenty-one, it is My sensations are *my* sensations. That is the mantra of the small astral body (the sentient body).

Sentient means sensitive, which, if you deal with adolescents, is also something pretty obvious. They are extremely sensitive, and what they are sensitive to is currents of feeling in the atmosphere. Somebody writes a letter to somebody, and within nanoseconds, the whole population of the high school knows about it. It is written in the hormonal cloud. There is some kind of molecular wave structure that they are all tuned to, and the small astral body is incredibly aware of what we could call the local weather reports—not so much a picture of what is over the hill, but what is happening right here between my skin and their skin. Every nuance is understood, but not in a cognitive way. But it is understood—emotionally. That's why gang hand signs, and paraphernalia, and Yo! and stuff like that are so inflammatory. It is a kind of tone language that says: We understand one another on this level of feeling.

The source of the forces in the small astral is the kidney. Biologically, the kidney is the perfect organ to be the source of the small astral, of sentience—sensitivity—because it runs a parallel track to the lung but in the opposite direction. They are going through the same anxiety and fear, but they are going through it in a polar opposite way. Yesterday we talked about the lung starting out as the digestive bud, then involuting, then rising up above the diaphragm and meeting a tube that has actually grown in from the outside of the embryo into the lung, creating an air passage. Then the lung, which really wants to be cloistered, contributes feelings like "I'm just a digestive organ. I just work here. Don't talk to me about responsibilities; I don't want to deal with it." That's the lung. "Just the facts, I'm just dealing with the dust of facts." We have seen where the lung gets pushed up into a realm where it doesn't feel so comfortable. That is the drama of the lung—and this is the drama of the child coming out of paradise, falling to earth and saying, "Responsibility? Don't talk to me about it; I'm still sore."

The kidney, in the embryo, starts as two organs in the realm of the ears and the eyes, up near the mandibles. There is a whole ring of little limbs that are vestigial organs that used to be the gills in the fish; that is where all the limb structure of the head comes out, the organs of communication, the jaw and larynx. It is right in that area that we could call the "communication central" or something like that—the organs that will eventually become organs of communication, which even includes input from the eyes. There are two little vessels that form the *pronephros*, the original kidney.

In the development of the embryo, the *pronephros* starts in the region of the ears. It then moves down through the body into the sacrum, where the pelvic bones are going to be. The kidneys go from being a sense organ in the head, somewhat equivalent to an eye and an ear, and maybe even a tongue—all this higher soul function—and then they descend into the deepest areas of the metabolic region in the embryo. This happens towards term, and then, just in the last month or so, they turn and make their way back up until they get caught in the loin. This is the place where we can turn, where we have flexibility in our spine. It is called the lower neck by older physiologists. They are looking for a place where they used to be to settle in. They go down and get so far down that they turn around and come back again.

This is very much the mood of the adolescent. They have just come down and they have been all the way down and they are thinking, "If I ever survive this, I'm going to be a millionaire and get a BMW and live on Maui. I just want to get a million dollars by the time I'm twenty and then I'll be all right." That's the big scheme, the big plan. That's what they write in their compositions: "My First Million." That's the hope of the kidneys. After they have been down in the bottom and they are on their way back up again, it is a feeling that, "Maybe someday I could actually become a sense organ again." You know it is a joke—but that is exactly what has to happen.

The adult has to make an equivalent in his or her soul of what the cosmos has created in the body. An organ must be formed which can perceive the spirit. It is called a chakra. The way in which we accomplish forming chakras is through what Rudolf Steiner called the turning of the soul. That is the next educational chapter. After the children leave you folks, they go somewhere. Yes, there is life after Waldorf! They go into the world, and then they get into the struggle of having to turn the soul. For that, they need organs for perceiving the spirit, and these organs can only be developed meditatively. Adolescents are sensing that necessity on the horizon, but they are still down somewhere near the bottom of the barrel biologically. They feel they have gotten a bad deal. They have come out of paradise and it has been x number of years of main lesson books and requirements; and now losing the basketball championship because I missed the foul shot; and girl-boy, mom-dad, job, college interviews, and grades; plus drugs, people on the street, and my best friend is now doing cocaine and I don't know what to say about it. This is a lot.

The musical forces in the small astral body are forces that Rudolf Steiner connects to the god Dionysos. In the lower school, it is actual speech and music per se. Speech and music—that is the healing force. That continues in the high school, but because of the expansion of the astral forces to such an enormous degree, Rudolf Steiner qualifies the term musical. If you read *Balance in Teaching* very carefully, when he starts to talk about the stages beyond the lower school into the middle school and beyond (he doesn't talk about the high school too much, but going into the middle school), he starts qualifying when he says musical. He says, "and I mean in the broadest sense." So yes, music and the arts; yes, they are healing in the curriculum, but there is this thing called truth, and it is a problem in the arts. If all we do is supply just more music and art, that will not heal this soul dilemma for the child in the high school by itself. Art will go a long way towards healing a lot of the things that adolescents have to deal with, especially pre-adolescent wounds, and things that happened when they were infants, but there is a special requirement that the high school teacher has. They have to bring the sense of truth, and that includes working in the arts. It is not simply making pictures anymore. The pictures must be extremely accurate in relationship to phenomena. That is the task of the high school. In the lower school it doesn't matter if the data is a little off. You can get a chance to correct it later. You have eight years to do it. But in the high school, you don't have eight years to do it; you just have your main lesson block. You go in, you do your block, and then there is the next block. That means when you present facts in the high school, they had better be able to be thought through by the student. This also can apply to seventh and eighth grade. Once they get into the middle school, this adolescent consciousness is very much beckoning. In some lower school classes, depending upon the constitution and approach of the teacher, this may happen. In fifth grade, there is a row of boys in the back reading *Scientific American* while you are talking about the gnomes in your botany block. Then they go home to their father, who is a rocket scientist at Aerojet, and say, "You know the sun isn't the center of the universe, according to my teacher." And there is a problem.

So as children move into the adolescent mood, they have a feeling for truth, which is the healing of the musical forces that are threatening to overwhelm the emotional life of the child with too much of the flute playing and dancing under the bushes of Dionysos. It is no longer just doing music. It is being *musical*. You have music class and you have learned to silent read; now it is notation and rhythm, and harmony. You need to come in at the right time. "You back there, you have to pay attention." It is that kind of consciousness in the arts—what we could call the discipline of the arts, or the technique of the arts—that has shifted in the high school. So it is no longer just living into the drama of the tone. They are already *filled* with the drama of the tone. They are reeking of it. What needs to happen is, "Okay, let's tone that down. It says in the score *pianissimo*, not so much *forte*. I know you like to hit the drum, but please come in at the right time and do what it says here." That is the whole battle in the high school—to try to present the arts as a discipline, as a technical discipline that requires practice and practice and practice. Then, if you get really good at practicing, in your twelfth year you can improvise, but only if you are good at practicing. Improvisation requires that you have that instrument down, *totally*. That is the challenge in the high school: to transform the arts, and the musical, and to weave them into the cognitive.

It is the same for a science teacher. I don't know if you have read the whole of *Balance in Teaching*, but in a certain spot Rudolf Steiner says some extremely disparaging things about scientists. He is really speaking about a prevalent scientific attitude that the scientist considers himself to be above the artistic, that the scientist has to work in such a way that the feelings don't enter in. The thinking is that the great danger of science as it is given to us, especially in an abstract way, is that the feelings have no place in it. The reason is that most of the feelings that are connected to the work in science have to do with feelings of the small astral that are formed in the kidneys. The most fundamental feeling of the small astral is, "I win." That's the basic feeling, because the kidneys are the source of instinctual patterns around issues of getting a mate, staking out a territory, guarding the harem, mother love, guarding the new infant, etcetera. Those are the feelings of the small astral—very deep, unspoken sensitivities flowing between souls. So the science teacher, or the math teacher, or the subject teacher, has a particularly strong challenge to take the data and the facts and to somehow enliven them with things like biography, so that the soul can take the facts of a particular person's scientific exploration and actually see that there was *a person* who did this, and that he or she had to struggle with personal feelings of inadequacy to do it.

That is very healing for the high school students—to learn that they are not the only ones who are suffering their brains out, and that the people who have given us great contributions are the ones that have done the most suffering—the ones who could hack it, as they say, the ones who could stay in the game when it was getting tough. The science lesson is most effective when it evokes a feeling that there is a wholeness in the phenomena that we are presenting in the science lesson—that everything that appears to be a fact is really part of a great process. That and biography are the keys to bringing the sciences alive. These approaches also help when the sciences become a problem in the sixth, seventh, and eighth grade. The facts are usually overwhelming, both for teacher and student, and if you eat enough of the facts, you become completely dead in your soul, unless you can bring musical forces of enthusiasm to them.

The enthusiasm lies in the experience that everything that is a fact is embedded in a process. It is an activity. There is meaning in the feelings and processes that are in these scientific facts. The facts as they are presented really come from beings, creative beings. Enthusiasm for these thoughts creates the most effective mood. It is a kind of a mood, even though the facts themselves are really daunting, that as an adult I can enter into these facts and bring to them a sense that someone has created this idea, has brought this into being. Someone has created the idea of the chair you are sitting in.

We could say that if we wanted a mantra for that, it would be: Everything that was made was made. So the science lesson is really a sort of John Gospel gesture that all the facts that we find originated somewhere in a being. They were the result of the struggle of a being to overcome something. There was a process in that. Out of the process they have left a trail of becomings that we can follow, and then what has resulted is called the work of Madame Curie or whoever. Then the science becomes much more artistic. It becomes warm and livable and active.

Those are the keys that I would like to leave you with today. I heard some comments from teachers that these lectures are all about music or all about pictures. My real purpose in coming here to be with you is to say it is never *all any-*

thing. It is *that* child in *that* moment, and how much you can be willing to prepare and prepare and prepare, and then in the moment speak to the child and forget everything that you have prepared. That is what the high school children are hoping that you can do—be there with the facts, but then meet them as a soul.

Adult Education

Lecture given February 24, 2000

Today I would like to share with you some pictures from the work of Rudolf Steiner that point in a direction that I feel is now in a gestating process in the anthroposophical movement, the work in adult education. Even though Rudolf Steiner College has been there for twenty-four years, somehow the work of educating adults into the anthroposophical worldview is, I feel, really just now starting to open in a way that it can be, as Marlon Brando said, "I could have been a contender." Somehow in anthroposophical adult education we have to be contenders. We have to, as they say in basketball, step up our game, because the defense is getting pretty heavy.

The next wave is really in the realm of adult education, and that includes continuing education for teachers as adults, both within the bounds of the curriculum and outside of the work of learning the curriculum. Somehow this is a little tiny babe of adult education that is just receiving ether forces now. It has taken a long while to gestate. While I understand the need for the continuing pedagogical education for teachers, it is my perception that if more teachers need to come to Waldorf education, they are going to come through the door of anthroposophy, not curriculum study. It is a rare person just off the street who is willing to make the sacrifices that a Waldorf teacher has to make physically, mentally, and financially. In order to have a capacity to make these commitments, there needs to be something in the soul that can turn towards a moral force that is living latent in the soul—a moral force that our culture does not support at all. Developing moral forces in the soul doesn't happen simply by getting a job coming out of college or high school. It has to be cultivated in a certain way, and there has to be a place where a different kind of thinking and a different kind of feeling can emerge so that the will can be turned towards the idea of a moral deed. There needs to be a place where fertilization and gestation, where the organs of the soul, which are so delicate in the adult, will be nurtured in just the same way that the atmosphere in the kindergarten nurtures the organs of the growing child. We could say that there is a child that is growing in the adult, but it is a cosmic child. It is an embryo of the Christ being. This spirit embryo needs to be nurtured in just the same way as a young child needs to be nurtured in the womb or in the kindergarten. There cannot be any other task in that nurturing process. There can't be any bottom line or professional expectation. The motive for educating adults simply has to be that the adult student is studying to nurture that Christ embryo.

The yearning to do this nurturing often awakens in the human soul in the period that Rudolf Steiner calls the sentient soul period, from age twenty-one to twenty-eight. Addressing the aspirations of the youth of the world, this task of nurturing the Christ embryo needs to come to birth in the anthroposophical movement as another continuing element of Waldorf education. At Rudolf Steiner College, the colleagues are dedicated to the work of adult education, but there aren't really many direct indications in the anthroposophical literature to guide adult educators other than the whole body of work in anthroposophy. The whole of anthroposophy is our indication for the pedagogy of the adult, and it is really a good indication.

Anthroposophy is just as effective with adults as the lower school curriculum is for the souls of children. It is just that, with an adult, there needs to be a kind of reversal of some of the processes, and the work needs to be given to the adult in complete freedom. There cannot be any bottom line or any expectation that this work is going to yield anything, or else the work is seen as coercive and this reduces its potential for soul hygiene. The work has to come out of that unique individual soul on its own moral initiative to unfold towards something that is higher than one's own self. No one can teach that, especially to an adult. It is impossible to teach profound truths. That is an alchemical saying. All we can do is provide an opportunity for people to explore the possibility that maybe someday they would like to move in a certain direction morally, to turn their soul.

That is the difference between the high school and adult education. In the lower school you are building a fire. In the high school you are more or less setting backfires. In adult education you are trying to teach adults how to gather kindling for another higher kind of fire. As teacher, you must simply know when it is the proper time to strike the spark. As there is a shifting, between twenty-one and twenty-eight, of the forces of the soul, so there must be a shifting in the technique or the modality of the adult educator. It is useful for adult educators to try to get out of the role of being authority figures with answers. If they don't, then they are laming the growth of the very organ they are trying to create. Between twenty-one and twenty-eight, the cosmic forces that were present in the young child have almost completely withdrawn from the forming of the body. They simply become a potential in the body that Rudolf Steiner calls the ego organization. That ego organization is composed of all the sheaths of the digestive organs—all of the mesenteries and connective tissues and outer pleuras and surface membranes of the liver and lung and the kidney and the heart and the digestive organs and the intestines and all of the absorptive tissue in the metabolism—all of the coverings of the nerves—all of the pleuras and coverings of the vascular system. This includes everything from the inside of your cheek to the inside of your heart. Everywhere there is a membrane in the adult, there is the activity of the ego organization bringing forces of the periphery into the organism as a kind of will thinking.

In the adult, or in the young adult, there is a shifting from the adolescent posture regarding sensation—which is My sensation is *my* sensation—to the posture of the adult (age twenty-one to twenty-eight), who is maturing to the life task, and whose mantra is: My sensation has *meaning* outside of what it means to me. My sensations come to me from a world that is already intelligent, that is already ordered, that already has rules, that already has laws, that already has behind it an immense doing. Between twenty-one and twenty-eight, what comes into the soul is an experience that "Everything that was made was made." Everything was made by somebody: the chair you are sitting in, the hall we are sitting in, all our clothes, all our food; it was all made. Between twenty-one and twenty-eight, the adult runs into things like fatherhood, motherhood, mortgages. Life questions arise. Can I afford to send my child to the Waldorf school? It may be that I'm a Waldorf teacher and I can't yet afford to send my kid to the Waldorf school. This is a very big issue between twenty-one and twenty-eight. It is, we could say, a moral dilemma.

The moral is the special realm of activity of the Ego. The Ego is a specialist at being aware of moral movements, lawful movements, lawful activity. The Ego asks: Is what I am perceiving lawful? Does it have meaning beyond the situation? Between twenty-one and twenty-eight, the maturing young person looks to others around and asks: What type of sensations do you think are moral ones? Instead of the posturing of the adolescent, there is a kind of a searching for the deepest impulses that I have in me—the ones that I really can't understand rationally yet, but which I know are there. When I look at these impulses, they seem to me to have meaning, but then I must turn to other persons in the world and say to them, "Is this what this means to you?" That other person may be a woman, a man, a friend, a partner, a spouse, but I must turn to someone and say, "Can I share with you these tender things that I feel coming up in me about why am I here?"

Adolescents don't ask why they are here. They think they already know why they are here; they wonder why you don't know why they are here. But then they start paying the rent. Then they have to pay for car insurance. Then when their friends spill beer all over the back seat, it is their car instead of dad's, and something changes. What changes is that they start to have what we could call a moral horizon. They see that somewhere in the future, on the edge of this great dark unknown, they are going to have to confess. They are going to have to be in the driver's seat. They are going to have to pay the bills. They are going to have to carry the load. As Mark Twain said, "When I was eighteen my father was the stupidest person on the earth. By the time I got to be twenty-one, it was amazing how smart he got." Suddenly, in three years he turned into this very wise person. We could say that that is the rallying cry of the sentient soul: Oh wow, right! There is life after high school! I never thought about it. I thought my life would kind of drop off the end of the earth at twenty-seven. Now I see I have to be a player for a lot longer, so I had better find people around me that I can rely upon so that when I tell them my innermost stuff they are not going to say, "Boy, what planet are you from?" That's the dance that I see in my classroom every day up at the College. "What planet are you from?" So they come in with all kinds of paraphernalia and gestures, and then after a year we all say, "Oh, we're all just humans. Oh cool! I got it now. We're humans. Yes! How did that happen?" So there is nothing like a very good dose of Rudolf Steiner to lead you towards the idea that maybe you are a human being. His work is designed to do that. We could ask ourselves then, between twenty-one and twenty-eight, what are some guidelines for the sentient soul?

Sentient soul means the sensitive soul. Sentient body means the sensitive body. During adolescence the consciousness of adolescents is tuned to how sensitive their body is under the impact of sensory impressions. When that sensory impression comes in, there is a kind of posturing that is an echo of a temperamental disposition. But by the time they turn twenty-one and the Ego is set free in the soul, the astral forces have already established a major beachhead, and they are arising from the metabolic organs with extreme regularity. The archetypal picture of that is sexual fantasy—yearning for experience that lifts a person back out of the prison that the astral body finds itself in. This is drugs, alcohol, sex, rock 'n' roll. It allows us to have access to a place outside the organism where we can begin to once again hear the music of the spheres. The problem is that there is very little freedom in it, when it is induced. But the yearning is to get outside the body. It comes about because, in the sentient soul period, the adult is beginning the task of transforming the life organs—the liver, lung, kidney, and heart—into soul organs of imagination, inspiration, intuition. That starts at the birth of the Ego at twenty-one. The life forces are given by the cosmos to children as a picture of the place from which they have come—the cosmos. Then the cosmic forces slowly withdraw; the astral forces and the Ego penetrate the lower part, the metabolic region of the organism as a will impulse, and then they start raying up from below.

The cosmic forces on the outside retreat up into the head. From there they look on the world, and what they are looking for in the world is the same type of ordering that is present in the cosmos. They look out from the castle there on the hill—the head—out at a world that could appear to be disordered when the consciousness is under the impact of the rising astral forces. The world, under the impact of the astral forces, appears kind of goozly and slippery and then the thinking forces come in and say,

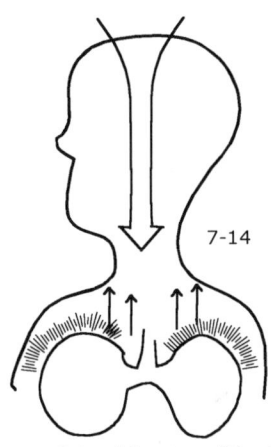

sculptural forces pull back as free forces rise off of the internal organs

"Oh, but there is meaning in that apparent chaos." That's the pulsation that happens in the sentient soul. There is a rising of the metabolic forces and a clouding of the consciousness in very deep feelings, very soul-felt feelings, and then a clarifying of that with thinking as a kind of oscillation in the organism between a dreaming consciousness and a day-awake consciousness.

The dreaming consciousness is very much stimulated by sensation. When sensations come in and start to impact the body, especially sensations having to do with the limbs, and the limbs being impacted by the musical forces (read: dancing and heavy music that just make the limbs throb with musical forces that rise up as a kind of a dream consciousness that takes the place of the painful quality of the day-waking consciousness), there is a kind of a dampening down of the day-waking consciousness. But when it happens synthetically, it no longer feels good. There is a kind of feeling like it used to be more fun when I didn't feel the consequences of this rampant astrality. So when you want to go out and have a six-pack of beer and a pizza at three o'clock in the morning and you can get up at five that same morning, things are fine when you are twenty-eight. But when you are thirty-eight, forget it. What is happening is that your conscience is telling you, "I would think twice about this." Eventually conscience has to develop under the person's own forces, according to cosmic plans. We are usually taught the hard way. This usually means learning on our own.

The picture of adult education is that these forces, these free forces that are arising in the adolescent, are joined by the Ego forces, and sensation becomes an outrageously entertaining experience. From twenty-one to twenty-eight, there is a craving for sensation—especially if the sensations that were taken in between birth and seven, and seven and fourteen, and fourteen and twenty-one did not satisfy the biological imperative. If those sensory forces did not satisfy the proper forming of the life organs and the endocrine patterns in the life organs, there is a yearning in the sentient soul period to go back to the spot where there was an itch, so to speak, and to try to relive those experiences, to rectify the perceived lack, and to bring that part of the subtle bodies up to speed with the intellect that is starting to move ahead. This happens because soul is finding itself more and more up in the grail castle of the head where, watching life, it keeps asking, "Whose life is this? Where did these little beings come from that are following me around here, calling me mommy and wanting peanut butter sandwiches? How did that happen?" This is the overture for the grand awakening. When that happens in the inner life, that is a call from the cosmos saying, "You need to work on this." As responsibility looms on the horizon, the sentient soul people of twenty-one to twenty-eight say to themselves, "There must be a meaning to this. Is it really just a tale told by an idiot signifying nothing, or is there something else?"

It is just this feeling that the anthroposophical youth movement is trying to address. The people who are in the anthroposophical youth movement are some of the most amazing people. I can tell you, when I was twenty-one, I definitely did not have the consciousness of some of these young people. It is amazing. It just floors you what these twenty-one or twenty-two year olds are capable of doing, and how they can cut through the stuff to reach out for real values in life. Yet at the same time there is great confusion about values. It is like "I can get any information you want on the internet quicker than you can blink, but I really don't know about this thing about commitment to others or about kids. You know, do you hit them or do you not hit them?" There is great confusion about stuff like that. Oh! I know, let's look on the internet and find out. Search: Hitting. You'll get information but it is not going to help you, because what is happening is that the proper imagination has to come from your Ego. Your Ego has to find out what is moral—the hard way, so to speak. But there are some signposts and some teachers. As adult educators what could we do? What could we provide to help young adults face the beasts residing in their souls?

This circle is a picture that I use often in Goethean studies class to try to describe the generic ego. (I know it is kind of an oxymoron to say that.) This is a picture of a group soul ego, a generic ego. Ego-endowed beings have in them a capacity to organize sensory input in an extremely flexible and yet extremely accurate way. So this is a diagram of the twelve senses. In a given situation, an ego being could organize, for instance, the sense of touch and the sense of balance and the sense of vision and the sense of the word into the constellation of *square*, and take all the senses that are in that

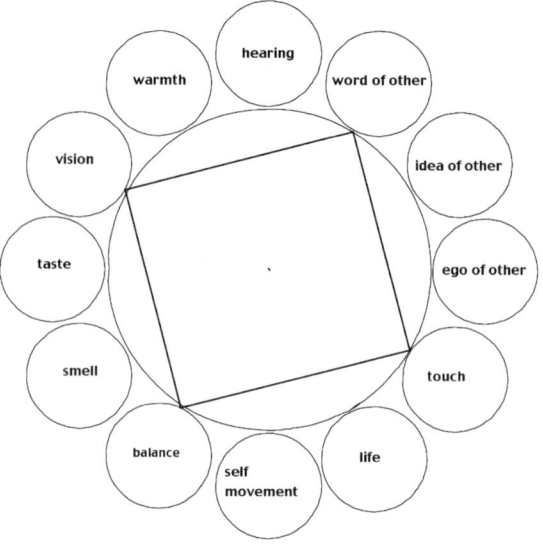

square and unite them in that one situation. Then at the drop of a hat, the ego could take senses which were not in that constellation, but were maybe trine to each other, and then bring those together. Or, maybe in a situation it needs to form an opposition of two senses. Bang! If you read about the senses by all the different writers in anthroposophy, each writer who has written about the senses will have a favorite modality. They will then say: This is the way Rudolf Steiner described the senses. If you take all of the various descriptions together, you have a dynamic picture of an Ego in action.

An Ego has a lot of options. It can *gestalt* and then change, just like that. If it can't, then it has problems. Or if one of the senses has been taken out of the mix when the person was five years old, then this Ego tries to form a trine using that sense as one of the key elements of that triangle, and what comes up is, "This is not available to you." Then that Ego experiences what we could call stress. It has to pull something from another sense and try to supply that in that trine in order to get a feeling of completeness, and then the situation gets muddled. Maybe the Ego is supposed to be hearing something, but it can't really hear it, so it flips into the sense of warmth or something else, and tries to find that in the hearing sense. It is trying to patch things up, whereas if it were really the being that it was designed to be in the creative lodge of the gods, it would have access to, and be able to play all of the senses equally like a keyboard or a palette. If you want to paint a picture, and every time you dip your paintbrush into green, something in you feels as though you are going to have to go do something crazy, then you are not going to use much green in your picture. But it may be that the green that you need to put in your picture is the thing that is going to heal you.

In the sentient soul period you need to know if you can't have green in your picture. If I were to go into the piano and take out every fourth key and then we would ask someone to play, it would be kind of weird. That is just what happens in the soul when the Ego tries to call on its resources for integrating senses, and something has dropped out of the loop. You go to hit that key—and it may be the very key that allows the whole chord system to change from minor to major—but it is missing and you wonder what happened. Hey, what key are we in? No one knows how it happened, and suddenly the soul is in a funky place. That is like going from being placid at the breakfast table to being a volcano at the breakfast table—bang—because Johnny, who is three years old, spilt the milk again. We don't know why, but it just punches our button. That's the learning that the young adults are going through, and then they come to class, and you don't know why they are in their body in class but you know something is going on in their soul.

The Ego is a force in the soul which integrates sensations. The sensations come to the organism through a system of what Rudolf Steiner calls sheaths. Every place where there is a sheath there is a field, which we could say works like an antenna. The sheaths pick up forces and activities and movements and then transmit them and amplify them in similar ways to what happens in our radios and telephones or in a crystal. So Rudolf Steiner talks about the crystallizing effect of the Ego. It takes in all different kinds of things and gives them a crystal-like ordering principle. It makes music out of noise. Not just sound. It makes melody. In order to allow that to really function in the sentient soul period of life, there are certain things that can be given to adults so that they can, on their own, work to have the Ego do this music-making.

One of the great keys is the study of proportion. Michaela Glöckler gave a lecture a couple of years ago in which she said the great task of the educator is to transform the forces of growth into the forces of thinking. She indicated that this is achieved through the study of proportion, because in proportion we compare one thing to another thing that normally wouldn't be comparable; and our soul and the Ego link the two in a cognitive activity.

For example, we have a line over here that is a certain length, and then we have a line over there that is another length. If I take my fingers and measure, I can see that this line is two times the size of that line. But in another reality this small line has nothing at all to do with the big line. They just happen to be on the blackboard at the same time. If we look at them as happening to be on the blackboard at the same time, then we get analytical science. It is just an accident. This line is here and that line is there. They are just two data points. This tendency of soul is the source of the disparaging remarks that Rudolf Steiner makes about science in *Balance in Teaching*. What he is saying is that, if we see everything as separate from everything else, it will never lead to a capacity of moral intuition in the soul. Everything will be experienced as separate from everything else. That includes the earth and the idea that the earth is separate from me. If it is just a bunch of forces, then I can trash it and there are no implications. This is the dilemma in the soul that is at the root of pollution and the ecological movement. We once again have to get back into the soul the idea that I have something to do with what is going on out there. If I only can see these two lines on the board as separate things, then my consciousness can't bring them together. If I see that the small one is in a ratio of one to two to the large one, then my Ego links the two in meaning. They have meaning. They are relative. They speak to each other. The meaning happens in my soul. It is not in these two lines. You bring meaning to these two lines. Then, as you bring meaning to these two lines, and you can perceive the meaning, your sentient soul is strengthened by its contact with the Ego that can unite them and get meaning out of it. The study of proportion and ratio unites the musical and the formal together.

In the Goethean Studies class we do projective geometry, sacred geometry, platonic forms, all kinds of drawing ratios; we have calipers that measure the golden section, and we are always looking at ratio and proportion in bones and in plants as the basis of the curriculum. It is a proportion-based artistic activity. Our artistic activities in Goethean Studies aren't for self-expression, but they are always aimed towards the discipline of the art that happens through the study of proportion. Even if you are a lower school teacher and you look at the curriculum, you will see that many of the things that you bring really come out of proportion. It could happen in a science block in the high school that along with the data that you bring, you study proportional relationships in morphology—like Darcy Thompson's *Growth and Form*, etcetera—classic texts in morphology that were really inspired by Goethe. Those can be used as a part of the high school curriculum. There are many things that can be done to enliven the sense of relation and proportionality as part of the scientific and artistic activity from the lower school to the middle school to the high school. That is one stream, a bit on the formal side, but it makes a nod towards music.

On the other side we have rhythm. This is the musical side, but it is making a nod towards the formal side. In rhythm it is not so much the proportion that we see but the idea that everything has a process behind it.

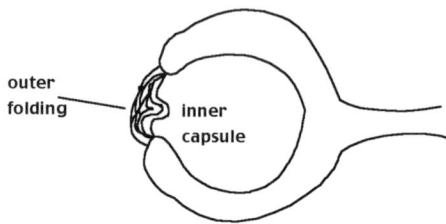

Here we see a diagram of the human eye in cross section. The eye starts out as two separate layers in the embryo. One layer starts to form a kind of capsule, and the other starts to fold in on itself. The outer layer folds in and the inner layer forms a kind of pocket. Layers keep forming and forming and forming. These are just layers of skin—membranes. Finally the skin on the inner side forms a pocket and the back of the pocket is lined with blood vessels. The skin on the outside forms a sort of scar tissue—layer after layer after layer—and that scar tissue is the lens. We have now a camera, but it is a camera that has arisen as a part of a process whereby the periphery and the center speak to one another.

That is where we started on Old Saturn, if you remember, with the Thrones and the Kyriotetes and the Spirits of

Motion. I have just been repeating that analogue rhythmically through time, again and again the same picture—again and again, so we could get now to this spot, having come from Old Saturn to Earth. Now we have to turn around and go back, but we are going to use the same analogue again as a picture of what we could call the breathing of the soul. The breathing of the soul is there in biology; everything has a movement from center to periphery, from periphery to center. We could call it an archetypal picture. It can be used as a meditative device. It is the equivalent of a verse, because in it there is an organized movement that the ego recognizes as being lawful. You can take anything in your physiology block and meditate the embryo genesis or the cytogenesis—the cell to tissue to organelle to organ system—and find that it fits the pattern of the Thrones, Spirits of Wisdom, Spirits of Motion.

If you take something like that and you begin meditating it, you will find that there will be insights in your inner life that start to lead you in the direction of process as a world phenomenon. If you then, out of that sense of process, begin to instigate a process, a rhythmical process of forming the image in the way in which you think you understand it (you could take anything to do this, anything in nature)—take it and try to form it inwardly the way you think it came into being, as a picture. When you do that, you are participating in what Rudolf Steiner calls the Christ language of nature. It is a picture of the lawful becomings now that Christ has united His Being with the Earth.

You take a picture from the natural world; you hold it and try to unfold it sequence to sequence. A picture will form in you as a process of becoming. When you do that, you have directly entered your etheric body; that is imagination. In the beginning it is an imagination with a small i. If it is taken as a practice—a regular, rhythmical practice—and again and again you form a leaf and try to see how the leaf would grow, growing it in your inner eye, that is a meditation. It is an etheric meditation on the formal principle behind the leaf.

If it is incorrect, and you keep persisting in the rhythm, it will be corrected. It will be corrected by the beings who stand behind those ether forces in the natural world. They will come to you because suddenly here is a human being who is showing an extraordinary interest in their activity. Just think how you would feel if you had been laboring your whole life to do something in obscurity, and suddenly some being poked his head through into the space where you were working and said, "Wow! That is really cool, what you are doing!" What would you do? You would turn to him and say, "Hey! Where have you been all my life?" That is just what the beings who are serving the Christ Being and the Hierarchies in nature will do when you start to pay attention to them in the way that they need to be paid attention to, which is in a lawful way.

Goethe called this practice *exact sense perception*. It is a great tool for the Waldorf teacher. Take anything that you are struggling with in a block, in a science block especially, and just try to picture it. But don't picture it as a dead thing; picture it with a sensitivity towards how it looked just before it got to where it is now. Then take that a step back, and then a step back. If you can get two or three steps back, you are in your ether body. That is right from Rudolf Steiner. You are in your ether body if you can begin to see this process inwardly in an exact way. It has to be exact—and there is a danger. The danger is that when you do that, and you start to actually see pictures, you will think: one, that you made them; and two, that they are correct. So we have to make that more rigorous.

What we do is to go from the ether body into the astral body, because the astral body is where the action is. That is where the adversaries are building little fast food places where they hang out, waiting for lunch time. We need to find a way in there, and the way we find in, which sounds paradoxical, is that *after* we form the exact picture we have to think it away into complete and utter silence. When we think it away into complete and utter silence, we have entered directly into our astral body, according to Rudolf Steiner. When we participate in the astral body, the danger is that in the astral body we have the experience that we have no form, because the form comes from the etheric pole.

When we enter the astral body, we have the feeling that we have no form. However, if you have engaged your will to form an accurate picture of a phenomenon in the ether body, and then you have rhythmically placed that in the stream of time in your will, every time you release the form that you have created, your astral body has an imprint from the etheric that has connected to it the force of attention in your Ego. There is a protection provided by you in that space where normally you would be dreaming in your astral body. Through the work in your ether body, you have suddenly brought the day-awake consciousness of your Ego into those ether forces, formed a picture, and released the picture backwards into silence. (This is the source of the backspace phenomenon for you eurythmists.) You release it into the backspace, and as that picture goes away from you, your ego can follow it because the Ego has invested will in the ether body, in the forming of it. If this goes into rhythm, then the ego starts to find itself, so to speak, in the rhythm, because what the ego is looking for is lawful motion.

You supply the lawful motion by having a practice that is regular. That is the grounding that the Ego is looking for, the regularity of the rhythm of the practice. You form the picture, you release the picture, the picture goes into the spiritual world—but it has a component in it of the day-waking consciousness, so that when it comes back to you as a memory, it comes back having been corrected by the spiritual beings that are connected to you. That is then called inspiration. What do you do? You try to form it again, to test it and correct it and see if it fits the phenomenon. So at every step of the way you want your Ego present, checking and saying, "Is this real, or is this just some kind of fantasy that I am receiving?" Fantasy is great from birth to seven, but after seven it gets us in trouble. After seven, those growth forces have to be transformed into the forces of thinking. But abstraction kills this process, because in abstraction we think we have solved the mystery.

So now we finally get to the title of these lectures, "The Death of the Mysterious." The normal education that is in the world seeks to solve the mysteries by giving us very rigid thought forms that have been thought all the way through in order to exclude the possibility that there is a larger consciousness than our own human consciousness. This is an evolutionary development. With the development of Ego and day-waking consciousness, this had to happen. But it is in certain ways hubris, a tremendous inflation, and we pay the price by being fearful in our daily life of the things we don't understand. We become fearful of mystery. We become uncomfortable in silence. We become uncomfortable if we are placed in a situation where we have no concrete knowing, because we ordinarily expect that surely *somebody* knows the answer! Maybe an expert will tell us what is true and what is not.

But that is an adolescent gesture. Adults don't need an expert; they need very clear counsel with their own soul. That is where it is best to search for answers as an adult. If we find the answers there first, we can go to any source—the

Internet, the encyclopedia, whatever—and we will find in that source the answer we have already received in our inner life. We may not have the facts in the way we need to get them, but facts can always be acquired. What we will have is an inner picture that will allow us to go to the fact that we need and see its meaning. In the future, my understanding is that availability of information will increase exponentially and we will not be able to come to a conclusion about anything. We older folks can already feel it.

You could take that feeling and multiply *that* exponentially, and that is the feeling that the young people have. They just all know that. Information is cheap and knowing is dear. Images are cheap and significant images are dear. Relationships are casual; significant relationships are dear. The young people are searching for the heart relationships and all they are given from the culture is data, access to data. If we don't allow them to see that the access to data is just trying to satisfy a craving—that the real access they need is to their own being, that the answers really come from within the research that they do and the work that they do meditatively on themselves—then they will go out in the world and just take icons that they can set up, and they will look for people who look at those icons and say, "Yes we all believe in this icon." That is the door to mass psychosis.

The young people that are coming out of Waldorf schools have been imbued with capacities that are really radically needed today. But when they leave the Waldorf school, and they go out into the world, and they try to bring these beautiful pictures that they have been given, they find that the world really doesn't have an interest in them. Then they turn inward, as they must. I would just make a plea to you teachers of the young ones. After they go out of your classroom, they haven't finished with their education. They go somewhere, and they need to be given a picture through you that you may not have all the answers, but that you have something going on inside you which allows that to be okay. Then they will grow up knowing that it is all right to be a seeker after the mysteries, and that it is all right to have mysteries in our lives, because mysteries really are the source of our spiritual growth.

Development of the Heart-eye

Evening lecture to members of the Anthroposophical Society, as well as to Waldorf Teachers, February 23, 2000

The subject of this lecture is the developmental stages of the human being. At the Waldorf Teacher's Conference, I have been talking about the educative process in children and how the cosmos forms organs in children, using the etheric as the formative principle. The law we have been exploring is that once the life organs are complete, then the cosmos withdraws and it becomes necessary for the human being to actually continue in a conscious way in the completing and forming of not only the physical organs but what we could call the organs of the soul. It is the formation of the soul organs, the chakras, in particular ways, that is really the focus of what I would like to speak about tonight, especially with regard to the dialogue with the guardian of the threshold. In the language that Rudolf Steiner has supplied for the lower guardian, there is a kind of primer, or road map, of the development of the chakras that you can find in many other places, most notably in a little book called *The World of the Senses and the World of the Spirit*, or in *Knowledge of the Higher Worlds*. In that book, there is a particular sequence of development that Rudolf Steiner describes, going from sensing and thinking, which is pretty much instinctual—which is the pattern in the young child—up through developmental stages where the human being is asked to develop the capacity to surrender to the requirements of his or her own destiny. That level of surrender makes of the human being a spiritual being among spiritual beings.

There are several notable steps in the process, and it occurred to me a couple of years ago that the steps that Rudolf Steiner gives in *The World of the Senses and the World of the Spirit* are very clearly defined in the language of the dialogue with the lower guardian. So what I will do tonight is to try to bring these two ideas together to show how in the descriptions that appear to be different in these books, Rudolf Steiner is really talking about the same thing. He is talking about a path of transformation involving the thinking and the senses, worked on consciously by an adult.

We could begin by saying that a person, once all the life organs are developed, by the end of adolescence, is pretty much complete. Also, the temperament is pretty much settled. Really there is nothing after the age of twenty-one to impel a person to develop any further. The cosmos has more or less finished its job, and the soul is left to its own recognizance. In many lives, that is about as far as the developmental task goes. Rudolf Steiner says very clearly that often whether one has the capacity for further development or not is based on karma. So, in many lives today, karma prevents a person from actually finding something like the Anthroposophical Society in which these ideas are freely shared among members regarding self-development—how to go through self-development, what we could expect, what the stages are, etcetera. The risks, the goals, even the techniques are available. It is not usual in a biography that a person would have access to that, especially the way in which it is presented in anthroposophy with such a rich body of knowledge and technique.

The work on the self forms the basic teaching in what Rudolf Steiner would later call the School of Michael. This is especially presented in the last part of *Anthroposophical Leading Thoughts,* where he is honing in on an idea about the whole problem of a human being's having sensation—and what that really does in the human, and what the twelve senses do to the human. The senses are pictured as keeping human beings in a kind of cocoon or web of almost dream-like states or, as Rudolf Steiner calls it in other places, urge and drive and instinct.

The senses that are locked to the physical body are what in the language of philosophy are related to the *problem of the given*. The given is what we experience through the senses, when we look out into the world or we listen to the things that come to us, to our soul, as complete, as given. For example: this is a complete podium. Out in the world there are flowers, people, chairs, a room, cars. All of them are given as complete in themselves. We accept certain parameters such as: we can't walk through walls. The world appears to us as, we could say, finished. It appears to the senses to be finished—in a word, given. Of course there are processes going on in the world, but, as far as our soul relates to them, we have very little control over those processes. If it is a thunderstorm, then it is a thunderstorm. We could try to seed the clouds or do whatever we will, and we may be able to gain a little foothold into controlling the phenomena, but basically the world of nature is a given world. As a result, the experiences that we have of the senses are that all that comes to us through the senses is given to us in a finished form and our responses are more or less programmed. All of the stimulus-response patterns in the endocrine pathways and all of that inner turmoil that happens as a result of sensation is also given. So we could say that in the realm of sensation, the human being is embedded in a universe of givens, or as Rudolf Steiner puts it, a cosmos. Cosmos means order, but esoterically, it means the given order. So the cosmic forces really are impelling us to have certain experiences, and the way in which we usually experience them as a human being is through the senses. Out of these experiences grows a mood. It is a mood that we could best describe as: The world is finished, so why bother? It is complete. I work on it; something happens. After I work on it, then immediately it starts to decay. So then I become Sisyphus, you know? I push the rock up the hill; the rock comes back down the hill; I push the rock up the hill again. That is the sense world. It is finished. It is here today, gone tomorrow. We have many wonderful sayings about that nature. It teaches us that, as Suzuki Roshi said, "Life is like buying a ticket for a ship that you know is going to leave the pier and sink." So that pretty much sums up the given of the sense world. It gives us a mood that this too shall pass, and from dust we come and to dust we shall return. All of those pictures are of that mood.

In *The World of the Senses and the World of the Spirit,* Rudolf Steiner describes a force available to transform that mood of the inevitability of the givenness of the world. He calls the force *wonder*. The capacity of a human being to begin to wonder at the world heals the problem of the death of the sense world as a given. There is a little space that opens up when we wonder about something, where we are not quite so sure that the given is as we understand it. It may be that the sensation is indeed as it is given, but our experience of it isn't actually complete as a sensation, because we don't understand where the given has come from. We experience what it is, but not what it is as *a becoming*, as a wholeness. When we try to develop a consciousness of the becoming of the given, immediately what rises up in the soul is wonder. How did it get there? How did it come to be like this? How is it that it is this way with you, podium? How did you get here? What were the ideas in the mind of the creators who made you?

Asking these questions, we have the inner experience of running out of knowing about the becoming of the podium. Now, many people have seen this podium, and many people have wondered what its creator had in mind. If you have a little bit of anthroposophical knowledge, it is perfectly obvious what this podium is; this podium is a larynx. So there is a secret mystery language in there somewhere that we speak, because we can now link this to a larynx. Now you are all wondering, what does this podium have to do with a larynx? It is in the way in which the form is arranged. It is here as a kind of a picture of what I am trying to do with my larynx to you—a living picture.

When we start to link up a little bit of an idea with the object, we start to perceive that the object had a becoming, and that behind the becoming there was an idea. We could call it a creative idea. Now, what that does is allow us to move away from simply experiencing the podium as a dead object, move into the realm of becoming, go inside ourselves and search inside for the idea. We find, "Hey, that's a larynx! That's the form of a larynx. Isn't that interesting?" The idea gives a soul movement to this "dead" thing. Without that soul movement, the podium is just a rebus of what it has become. Contacting the becoming of the podium gives us a little breathing space inwardly, when we can bring a living concept to the dead percept and unite them. Something happens in the soul and we get expansion in our capacity. The expansion in our capacity is the basis of soul transformation. When we do that, we link a living idea to a percept, something is born in the soul that Rudolf Steiner calls *awe*. We become aware that this podium has a symbology and is not just a random thing, but that it has intelligence behind it. Not only that. If you really go into it, there is a deep esoteric significance to the way in which the form has arisen.

However, when we move into that realm of the concept behind the podium, there is also a given there. The given is the idea. Behind the podium is the living concept that is behind the human larynx. Once again, we have run out of knowing. Just as we had no knowing of how the podium came into being, we really don't have a knowing about the way the larynx came into being. But as we move inwardly, and we start to see the idea connect up to the outer phenomenon, then something arises in us of the two moods of wonder and awe, and suddenly we are not quite so sure that the world is as air-tight as we once thought it was. We begin to question the primacy of the given. We start to wonder about things—and the world starts to be permeated by what we could call mysteries. As the world starts to become mysterious, the soul begins to open towards the mystery because it feels inside itself that the mystery has something to do with its own development. We feel it has something to do with me. It is not just stuff out there any more. I'm the one who is allowing the percept and the concept to be united. Even though they are both given, there is something that is bringing them together, and that something (or really someone) is the I-being, the one who is engaged in the activity of knowing. The knower who is in the act of knowing is a special being, and we just come into the very edges of the active knower when uniting the percept and the concept. This is a wonderful experience, but as it happens there is also a danger.

The danger is that into the space of wonder, where we can say to ourselves "Maybe things are not the way I have thought they are," as we begin to open to this thought in freedom, right into that space comes the beast of doubt. Once you find that the world is a little "wiggly," it starts to unwind a little bit. If you read Rudolf Steiner, "wiggly" is a regular experience. That is, deeper knowledge is kind of wiggly, because just when you think you understand something, you pick up a new book and realize that you don't understand it at all. But Rudolf Steiner wrote that way consciously to prevent dogma. Think how much more dogma we would have if he hadn't done that. That's a frightening thought. He consciously tried to undogmatize the immense gifts that he brought, because he understood their power. So when the human being is working on consciously uniting this duality of the thought world and the sense world, and it becomes part of the capacity of the person to actually wield wonder and awe, then out of that comes the challenge of doubt. On the heels of insight comes the beast of doubt—mainly self-doubt.

The healing of doubt is accomplished through what Rudolf Steiner calls *enlivening the senses*. In the evolution of the human being, the senses have fallen out of creation at an early stage. They used to be organs that had life. When they were organs that had life, in the perception of objects or beings, the sense organs (according to Rudolf Steiner's indications) would actually perceive the *life* of the being, not the corpus of what it had become. That was the original plan anyway, until we were tempted in a certain way to give that up so we could have a sure and conscious knowing of *"that,"* so that we could say, "I am seeing 'that'." When "that" happens in our consciousness, we become aware of "that" object or being as a corpse and no longer see its life. The soul falls into doubt. Then the sense world and the senses themselves cease to work in an active living way, and they simply become prone to what Rudolf Steiner calls the laws of nature operating in the senses: the eye works simply like a camera, the ear is built simply like the strings of a piano. The human being has no real consciousness of the optics of the eye in the actual act of seeing, unless there is a pathology. When there is a pathology, we become aware that something is not right in the apparatus. Our consciousness, in that awareness, enters into the apparatus, but if it is working fine, we have no awareness of it. In order for it to be working fine, there has to be no life in the sense organ. If there is life, the organ itself starts to have its own activity, and we become aware of its activity rather than of what we are seeing. In order for us to actually see, there needs to be a damping down to almost the level of death of the activity of life in the senses.

We project that death process on what we see so that it becomes, as an alchemist would call it, a corpus. It is just a dead body. A "that." The same goes for thoughts. Rudolf Steiner says that any idea which does not become an ideal slays forces in the soul. So thoughts can become corpse-like also. The human being is living among the dead: the dead thoughts, the dead concepts, the dead sense world. The dead senses themselves, the organs themselves, are virtually devoid of life. The struggle to practice seeing Goetheanistically, which is trying to see the process of the becoming of whatever it is that we are observing, over time, over time, over time, allows a person to unite a percept and a concept in the activity of perception as it is happening, and to be able to observe the way in which the life of the organ is impacted by the sensation. That is fundamentally the goal of Goetheanistic work. When we actually do learn to see processes, there is a part of the soul that relates more to the process that is being perceived than to the object itself. It relates more to the activity of the becoming of what is thought than to the thought itself. In that way, there is an enlivening of the thinking and of the sensing that comes together in a living perception of the becoming of the archetype which stands behind the corpus. We actually perceive that this form *was made*, and that "everything that was made was made," and indeed it is not finished. Everything is an ongoing work.

That capacity in the soul life is then known as participatory consciousness. It is a form of magical thinking. With capacities like that in the soul, the thinking and the sensing start to live in a different way. There is a different gesture in the soul towards life and towards what life is bringing to us in the realm of thoughts and perceptions. This challenges the soul to move in a direction where, if you do these practices, you become aware that, simultaneous to the arising of a perception of the becoming of something, there is a feeling that you have done this before a million times. It is a feeling like, "I am still not out of prison even though I am perceiving becomings." This amplifies, with continued practice, into "When I am perceiving becomings, I am alive, and as soon as I reflect on having perceived the becoming, I am dead again." It is a definite feeling. The feeling is something like, "Who the heck made this system anyway?" As soon as I awaken to a reality at a certain level, and I cognize my awakening, I turn into a corpus. It is a very frustrating feeling, because in the moment of the becoming, the experience is exhilarating. As soon as it has become in me and I notice it, the experience loses its transcendent quality. It has lost its mystery; it has been depleted of its potential and its archetypal activity and simply becomes a "that" among other "thats." The feeling is that somehow in my soul I must not be doing something right.

Rudolf Steiner talks about this. You've read all the books; you've meditated for twenty-five years, and you have never had a pillar of fire talk to you, not even once. Why not? You want to know *why not*! That is a feeling we could call esoteric alienation. We feel alienated from the spirit. We feel, we could say, out of harmony with the phenomena of the world. When the world turns into a prison of "thats," we don't sense that everything is connected to everything. We realize that even the so-called corpses themselves are only corpses because I *believe* they are corpses. But if Christ had the perception that the corpse was the end of it all, there would be no Easter. He didn't have that perception at all, and, to my understanding, that is the great mystery teaching.

The bringing of new life into the corpus once again is the higher level of the great work. Once we enliven the senses, then we begin to be aware that all bodily organs are also corpse-like, that a large part of who I am—the part that I really value when I look in the mirror—is really not me and is eventually going back to its maker. It doesn't have much potential. That is a sobering thought, because it is such a wonderful, complex instrument. But it is only wonderful because the beings that made it are extra-super-wonderful. They made it, and they are maintaining it, and they want it back. There are just a few instructions in the owner's manual for optimal maintenance that we need to pay attention to. Be not mistaken; they *are* maintaining it. We take it into the shop every night, and they vacuum the rugs out and detail it, and it comes back in the morning, and there it is all shiny again. Well, there is some wear and tear and depreciation, but that is in the contract; it's amortized in, so there is not really a problem with that.

When we actually take on the challenge of trying to rectify our thinking and our sensing, the first thing that hits us is, "Wow, there is a lot more work to do to make this happen than I ever thought." Even though the instrument I have is so wonderful, I have, through my affiliations and my relationships to Lucifer and Ahriman, embedded that instrument with matter to such a degree that suffering is inevitable.

The original plan did not include suffering, according to Rudolf Steiner's picture in *The World of the Senses and the World of the Spirit*. There was another picture of what the physical body should be. In the Middle Ages, the word *substantia* meant the activity of the hierarchies working with each other. Today, it is the equivalent of "stuff." The shifting of that consciousness is the shifting towards materialization of the spirit, which Rudolf Steiner is warning us about all the time. So when people begin to work on themselves, especially their thinking and their sensing, the first thing that usually arises in the wake of that is the feeling that somehow what I am doing is not quite adequate. It needs to be worked on; it needs to be brought up to speed. My ether body needs to be quickened, or my astral body needs to be slowed down, or my ego needs to stop impacting so hard, or maybe it is hanging out most of the time and we need to tuck it back in. These are real feelings. These feelings are the sources of pathology. We have unsettled the subtle bodies, with the help of Lucifer and Ahriman.

An anthroposophical physician will say that what I am describing now is what Steiner gives as the basis for illness; it is the misalignment of the subtle bodies. As you work on yourself in this path of seeing becomings, you begin to see yourself as a becoming, and you begin to see the spots that have potential for becoming, but simultaneously you also see the spots which have somehow walled themselves off from becoming. We call them neuroses and syndromes in the soul and tumors in the body. Those are parts of the organism that have become habituated to fear and doubt and feeling out of sorts, feeling out of harmony. In the soul realm, doubt is the problem of thinking. The tendency to blame others is the fundamental problem in the middle realm of the feelings. When we start to take our own development in hand, and we see what comes up and we are not happy campers with it, the response to that is, "Look, it's not my fault; I've had a rough life." Or maybe, "The devil made me do it," or, "I got a bum organism from my parents," or, "I get a bum rap from my parents," or, "If only I were more beautiful, I wouldn't have these problems," or, "If I were only smarter," which is really saying that someone else needs to bear this—not me—

because I am doing my work. Here I am, working on my thinking, and I am working on my inner self and I am working on my senses and I am doing my Goethean exercises, or whatever, but this yuck that is coming up, this is somebody else's stuff, because it is too big for me to say it is mine. So we go around, and as our inner life develops, we see into the abyss of being. One day we have the experience that when someone does something, we say, "Oh yeah! Boy, that one is gonna hurt tomorrow." That is what Rudolf Steiner calls mocking. Or, "Oh boy, look at those shoes; where did you get those?" Mocking. Or, "Boy you are going to regret that you said that in this group!" Mocking. It happens a zillion times a day just as a flash. We think that when Rudolf Steiner says mocking, he really means going up to somebody and saying, "You are whatever." But it is really this subtle rising up of the feeling that "They are not me and that is so weird and I can see how weird that is, and so I'm just going to pass a judgement." Mocking is a mood of "They are not me, and I am not to blame, so they must be to blame." That is the second beast speaking in us.

Out of that mood of mocking comes the sense that "I could be in harmony if this or that person was not in this group or in this position. If they weren't here, this would be a really great place." What we are really yearning for is that everything be NICE, that everything be harmonious, because we remember somewhere in our spiritual biography that we used to live in a place where it seemed pretty nice. Then we came down here, and then things happened, and now we don't know who is to blame, but we are sure it is not us, and so we are hoping that maybe somehow our karma will allow this person to go away—not hurt them, just go away, go find a great job somewhere else. That is mocking, because basically what this is saying to our own soul is, "There is not much harmony in your life the way it is. The way your life is, is not okay."

Rudolf Steiner is very interesting in this regard; he said that if there is something that has come to you in your life, and you have a very profound wish that it be otherwise, you don't have the strength or capacity to learn the lesson that it is bringing. That is the way he puts it, and that is pretty fierce, because that opens the door to a lot of weird stuff such as "Whatever comes to me needs to come to me and it is coming from a higher place." Working with that thought can become pretty scary, because if I really really believe that everything that is coming to me is coming from a higher place, I can't blame anybody for anything! I just have to watch it, and watch the way I respond to it, and out of that comes the capacity to have the feeling of being in harmony with world phenomena. That is then what we could call the ensouling of the life forces. We once again *bring our soul into our life*. Somewhere along the line we learn to shut the soul out of our life because having it there is too painful. We make a few mistakes, and twenty years later: Oh my goodness how did that get here? One mistake and the whole world goes nuts. That is the tension we live in, in the inner life, when we undertake the task of working on ourselves. When we are actually good anthroposophists and we are doing the work and we are doing the exercises and we are reading the books and we are going to meetings and we are meeting people and we are striving, what starts to come up is, "Oh my god! My life is really weird." It is not harmonious at all, and I came here thinking everybody here was clairvoyant and we were all going to be harmonious. You know, that is what I was told before I came here: Everybody in the College at Sacramento is clairvoyant. It scared the life out of me to come here, I can tell you.

So when we actually start taking ourselves to task and working with these things, then we come in direct contact with the parts of our life forces which don't have soul capacities. They have been shunted off, they are sort of on automatic pilot, and it is in those automatic parts where pathology eventually starts. Soul pathology first, and then physical pathology will follow. They are islands of neurosis. That is how Freud described them. They are islands that get separated off from the flow of our life. The life organs are one of the key places where that happens, because they are the basis of temperament.

As we start to work, and as we start to unravel these mysteries of temperament in ourselves, we see our temperamental disposition. We can see the parts of ourselves that are less than wholesome, the parts that we would rather not have there, but there is a strength that builds in the soul to tolerate this level of seeing. The strength comes from the dialogues with our guardian. The guardian says to you, "You have created this, and I am here to tell you that." You can't say to him, "That belongs to somebody else. I'm sorry, you got the wrong shadow there, the wrong double." When we begin to have those experiences, and we begin to dialogue with other people on anthroposophy, and we start to develop some sort of practice, and we do art forms that start to pull out these qualities and bring them up into consciousness with regularity, it may appear that our life starts to unravel at the seams, but it is only the parts that are stuck that start to unravel. In actuality they are simply becoming more flexible. They may be ugly, but they are unraveling because they need to unravel in order for our soul to enter into the eternal life. And, if we are consistent, and we keep working, then we come upon the last challenge of the beast of fear which lives in the will.

Rudolf Steiner characterizes will as the place in the soul where we are totally asleep. It is relatively easy to change a thought that you find is erroneous. It is a little more difficult to change your feeling. Somebody does something to you and a feeling comes up, so you go and sit down and do whatever you need to do to turn it around and ten minutes later you come back. "Pins and needles, needles and pins; it's a happy man that grins." Remember that old one? So you can do things to kind of short-circuit strange feelings and cool them out and bring yourself back from mocking. But suppose there is an impulse in the will, in the habit body, and you say to yourself, "No I'm not going to do that." Then you are sure as shooting set to do that, because we have no access to impacted will forces with the forces of thinking. We have no access to it with the forces of feeling either. It is THE WILL, and we can't think about it because, as soon as we do, we fall asleep. We can't really enter into the feelings with it because, as soon as we do, we start dreaming about things, which leads to desire, and then pretty soon we are in trouble again.

The real transformation of the will is a difficult thing. Where is the handle? If we have some capacity for wonder, if we have some capacity for awe and feeling in harmony, then in the soul we begin to see into the great mystery of what Rudolf Steiner calls the level of the will in the Ego. The level of the will in the Ego is the capacity for people to see the motives behind what they are doing, because the level of the will in the Ego is motive. If we have a feeling of harmony with world phenomena and we know we can't blame anyone for our misfortune, then we can actually watch our misfortune coming towards us as a known pattern, and we can be aware of it and embrace the blame structure which is really a kind of resistance to what is coming. If we can manage to simply turn the blaming around so we can say to ourselves, "Yes, it wasn't the most wonderful thing I ever did but yes, I see that in my soul I want to really be in harmony with world phenomena." This allows us to see into the sleeping giant of our will.

Rudolf Steiner describes this process of seeing into will as the ability to say there was another being in us up there on the roof that pushed the tile off the roof that hit us in the head that woke us up, and that that other being up there is the higher person in us. When we see into motive in the will, we understand that there is a better person in us. When we can see in ourselves that there is a better person in us that is actually working with hierarchies to create situations where we get smarter and more awake and more in harmony, that is what is known as the turning of the will. The turning of the will allows us to accept the destiny patterns without flinching, and to be able to take the blows of destiny and to transform them into a capacity to do things we came into life to do. It is a great alchemy in the soul in the level of the will.

We all know the situation where we go through some horrible thing in our life. I like to tell the story of how submarine boot camp was the pits for me. It was the worst. It was horrible when I was in it. I would go home over the weekend and tell horrible stories. But now they are my *best* stories. You would think I had a ball then! It has gone on in me, and I see the wisdom of having to suffer those things, and I can include that experience in my soul life without feeling that it was the worst thing that ever happened, because now in my soul I have the will to accept that that was part of my destiny. It only took thirty-something years, but that is the way the will works.

The turning of the will is very slow, but when it happens, the turning of the will develops the capacity in the soul to surrender to one's destiny. It is not surrendering out of weakness; it is surrendering out of knowledge that what is given is given to us for the betterment of the whole, and that nothing is given beyond our capacity to understand, and that if we work our way through it that there is always a lesson. We learn to trust that if we go through it, we come out on the other side a better person. Somehow, magically, we receive forces from the cosmos to become a better person, to have more resilience or more flexibility or to become more allowing or more capable of love. We see that we can become larger than we used to be. It is just the willingness to accept that maybe there is a higher order or a even higher being in us who has designed our life to be exactly the life that we need to lead in order to serve the rest of our fellow human beings. Rudolf Steiner calls that surrender. It is not out of weakness at all; it is out of the turning of the will towards our destiny. Now when that happens there is a force in the soul that arises that we could call love.

Love is the willingness to undergo what needs to be, because we see that it needs to be. That is what eradicates fear. If we have some capacities, we can pretty much say, "If I do that, this is going to happen, and I don't think I really want to do that." So we are free. We don't *have* to do anything really, but if we have a capacity which allows us to surrender, we might be able to do the thing that is not the thing that we would normally do. No one forces us; no situation forces us, but we find in ourselves a capacity to surrender to our destiny.

Now, when we are doing this work of self-transformation, it doesn't always go click, click, click, because we may be on one level with one issue and on another level with another issue. We may have worked through ice cream or something along the way, and gotten up here into the realm of will with it, where we can actually start to turn the will and see all kinds of patterns coming out of ice cream, but we haven't quite gotten to chocolate yet. That's later. It's not click, click, click, but it is polyrhythmic and polyphonic. It is woven.

In the weaving of all of these forces, we can have the experience that somehow in the mystery of it all, in the maintaining of the mystery of the human being, when I surrender my will—or in my will I find the capacity to surrender to my destiny—my will becomes like a kind of thinking. My deeds start to somehow make sense in the big picture. They become ordered and not random. We see the patterns. When I do this, that happens over there. The will nature becomes more like thinking. We see patterns of becoming and relationships. When the will nature becomes more like thinking, that is called karma research. We actually start using our will to look into the stream of time as a kind of thinking organ which only thinks in time. With this will organ we start to see patterns unfolding. We realize that there is meaning in all of this. My life is not just total chaos. This includes the big questions about evil and injustice. Our soul gets much more capable of not blaming in injustice, but simply trying to separate out things, and then giving the judgement to a higher place.

As the will becomes more like a thinking organ, simultaneously the thinking becomes more will-like, because we can actually think about something that we want to think about, instead of drifting into lunch or something. We actually can take the thinking and will it. We can place something in the field of thinking and then do it again and again and again. If we want to keep that thing in the field of thought, we will it in time, to move through time, and eventually we see the whole of this thing which we normally would only see as a little piece. We start to see wholes.

This then is Goetheanism. The thinking has a will component. When those two forces are developed in the soul, then the feeling in the middle realm becomes what Rudolf Steiner calls *gemüt*. It is probably the most mysterious element that is in the work of Rudolf Steiner—probably the most misunderstood—that somehow the heart has an eye which opens when the thinking and the will come together. When the thinking and the will come together, the eye of the heart opens and begins to see reality just as it is, without blaming, without judging others. It simply becomes, as Emerson put itt, a naked eyeball observing the universe.

My understanding is that this heart-eye, the development of the heart-eye, is really the goal of the anthroposophical working. It is not a head path. All we have to do is look at all the farms and schools and clinics and whatever, and say it really is a will path. But then we look at all the books and we say, well really it is a thinking path. But if we look at everybody sitting here next to each other, and we all think we are all here because of the work of Rudolf Steiner, then it becomes a seeing with the heart, and each of us can then see each other as brothers and sisters in the great mystery school of anthroposophy.

APPENDIX A

Questions and answers following the lecture on Developing the Heart-eye.

Q: Would you say that the development of an awareness of the process is the process of the teacher, or is it that where we are all going is to become our own teachers?

A: That awareness of the awareness, in my understanding, is known esoterically as the witness. There is, in this work, a capacity to develop the ability to see your soul engaged in soul processes. It is in the realm of the *gemüt* that the witness really has its focus. It is to look with the eye of the heart at the potential of things. Rudolf Steiner says to the teachers: Don't look at the child; look at what the child can become. Don't look at people; look around them. Place your attention around them. When we practice that, we develop a capacity in ourselves to watch ourselves do things. He says in many places: Learn to get outside your body and look back at it. When we do that, we become coherent outside the body. We have the same experience outside the body as we had in the body, but we know we are outside. Then we begin to live as citizens in the cosmos through this action of the witness. It is a kind of grace, as I understand it, that comes as a result of the work. My understanding is that you can't really sit down and say: I'm going to develop the witness. If you do the work, and you go through the process, then slowly a kind of a grace reservoir, or a bank of forces, builds in you as a capacity whereby suddenly you know when something is about to happen. It usually happens when you are about to say something that is going to get you in deep trouble. Rudolf Steiner calls that the capacity to see the karma of a deed as you are doing it.

Q: You mentioned that the surrender of the will leads to a turning of the destiny, that we really see our destiny. I really agree with that, and I would say that there is another stage beyond that—that the destiny actually changes, and that that is really a part of the karma research—that we then see that karma is possible not only to be a given that we surrender to, but also needs to become something malleable, out of breathing with the Hierarchies, and I wonder if you could speak about that.

A: Yes. That is really really in the future. Theoretically I say yes. I can't get my soul around it. Theoretically I would agree, but I haven't been able to live it. Karma for me, especially in the way Rudolf Steiner presents it, leaves me with the feeling that I have a karma blinder in my life. It is just a mood. I haven't done a lot of research in the idea of changing one's karma.

Q: When I look at the Mystery Dramas and really live into those characters, I see this malleability quality coming in certain characters. I'm just saying that I think there is another stage that happens.

Q: You spoke about the school of Michael being connected to the problem of the human being having sensation. I wonder if you could just say a little more about that.

A: Yes. In *Anthroposophical Leading Thoughts*—at the end—Rudolf Steiner talks about many different aspects of the problem of the transformation of the sense life, and that through thinking we can actually begin to rectify the currents in our soul—that thinking is one of the soul forces, feeling is one of the soul forces, willing is one of the forces. We can work on them and then there becomes a capacity to work on ourselves. But the senses themselves, and the way in which we are arranged in the body of the senses—the fields of activity around them—are still really in the hands of the Hierarchies. But what has happened, due to the temptation and the Fall, is that we have brought things into the realm of sensation that are not really part of the original picture. The Hierarchies don't know what to do about this issue because it is not part of something that they really work with. Tragically, we don't know what to do about our sensation because we are really busy working on thinking, feeling, and willing as a lower level mystery school. So there is an untransformed residue left over from our mystery training as it stands in the world today. Rudolf Steiner is very clear: everything gets transformed. If there is one atom left over that doesn't get transformed, Ahriman wins. So that means your eyeball, your Cadillac, whatever; it all has to get transformed back into spirit. In the realm of the senses, the need to have that Cadillac be in that parking lot when you leave here is a problem. We could call it soul pollution or the pollution of the "I" in the higher realms. In these realms we now have all these things going on that lead to the illusion of a separate self. The senses which contribute to that illusion need to be redeemed. They need to be transformed. The mood I catch from Rudolf Steiner's work is that the rest of the Hierarchies are saying, "I don't get it." They say to the creator, "We gave them all this great stuff and look at what they are doing with it. They are following these retarded beings who made spirit fall into matter. Why are they doing that?" Then they ask us, "Why are you doing that?" and we say "I don't know." But if we start to work on ourselves, Michael will just keep saying, "There it is. There it is; work on it. Go for it. You have to redeem that. We have a great teacher in the Christ who has come back and done that. He has transformed the physical into spirit." But the rest of us are still trying to understand that deed. Michael is here to remind us to try to do that. He has a school. In the school you learn that that is the way it is, that the sense world is just the thing you need until you find that you don't need it, and then when you realize what you have done, you are going to have to transform the sense world and bring it all back into the spirit. You will then be the tenth Hierarchy as world creators in the imitation of Christ.

Q: Earlier you mentioned grace. Probably everybody over seventy thinks that Rudolf Steiner once said that when you are over seventy you live by grace, and sometimes you wonder. Maybe you have to be over eighty-five? You have to have time to look back on your life and say, "Oh that happened so I would see this, and that happened to give me this challenge, that happened to give me this capacity," and then it can be quite wonderful if you can overlook the physical problems.

A: Yes, you can overlook the physical problems. It is the physical where it falls. That is what we have to bring back again into life, and so grace comes.

Q: I'm interested to hear you talk about blame. It seems to be such a habit in our times, and I'd like some indication on how to research that idea in Rudolf Steiner's work. I don't recall coming across it in those terms.

A: Blame is mocking, the second beast. Mocking in the broadest sense, as I understand it, is the tendency to see everybody else as different from me. That's mocking. We do it all the time. We are driving down the road and some guy drives by in a blue Cobra with flames and big slicks on the back and we think, "Oh he probably got it on welfare." In that thought there is blaming. We are really saying: He is to blame for my taxes. He is on welfare. He buys cigarettes and gas for his car with my money. We don't quite go that far, but that is the gesture. When we see that in our lives, it appears endless. It is kind of everywhere. We have a culture of blame. It just means that somebody else did something and he is the one who is wrong.

Q: Just to make a distinction, aside from saying that everyone else is at fault, you can also do the opposite and say that it is just me that is at fault. There is a quite a distinction between blaming yourself and taking responsibility.

A: That's correct. That's right. Whether the blame is out or in, it is still pretty widespread. Taking responsibility or owning the problem means saying: Yes, I did it, but I'm not going to blame myself, I'm just going to say yes I did it and watch. That is witnessing. I'm going to witness what happens. And immediately a tape goes in: Somebody's got to be to blame. But that is what the adversaries bring. Somebody has got to be to blame, and we are going to find out who it is. That voice is not really us, because in that attitude we don't take responsibility. Earth can really be an ugly place sometimes, because something will happen and you will have some knowing about what happened, and there will be nothing you can do because you have already made a vow to yourself that there is no blame, and you have to turn that thing around in your own soul. It is called cooking and eating the shadow. That is an alchemical term. Shadow is an acquired taste, I might add. But you can acquire a taste for it.

Q: How do you instruct about blaming without going too much into the head? How can we stay in the feeling realm?

A: Don't discuss blaming; just don't do it. Sit down with the other person. Talk to him about possibilities for problem ownership, but try not to blame. Blame is not part of things we humans should do with one another. If you have a problem with me, please communicate your problem to me without blaming me. I'll give it back to you as I think I heard it, and you can correct my error, and I'll give it back to you until you are satisfied that I heard you. By then I'll probably have a problem, so I'll have to tell you what my problem is, but I'm not going to blame you because you didn't blame me and because I know you are going to tell me back what you heard and so on. We can tell each other what we are really unhappy about without blaming, and both of us come out of that feeling like we were heard. Nobody has to blame anybody, and yet everybody has been heard, and people in themselves find the capacity to turn their soul or make amends. They say, "Well yeah, maybe I shouldn't have done that." Whereas if you get to the meeting and say, "You did this!" They are going to say, "I didn't do it, they did it" Blaming is really just a language thing, and new language can easily be learned. If you go to marriage counseling or family counseling, that is what they will teach you how to do—how to share your concerns without blaming.

Q: Forgiveness can also fit into what you are saying right now in sort of a natural practice which brings together all the thinking and also the willing, as a sort of a harmonizing of the two elements in the practical sense of practice that brings one into a reconciliation with ourselves, and a reconciliation with one's destiny, and a reconciliation with one's community.

A: Thank you, that is a nice point.

Q: I don't see how it can work that human destiny unfolds in the right way with all of these billions of people on the planet, when all these billions of people have free will to go against the godhead, which means that maybe I wouldn't be what was planned in the life of another person. Part of you says to trust in what comes, and part of you doubts what needs to come. Another part says it is impossible that this can even work.

A: Yes, but I think a useful picture was given in the last point. Read St. Paul in Corinthians about love. With love there is nothing impossible. With forgiveness, things can change. Jacob Boehme said that the human heart is deep. It is mysterious. It is unfathomable. Out of that fountain of the human heart comes forgiveness and love and the capacity to look for reconciliation. Forgiveness is not logical. It is not really thinkable. But it is doable. That is a great mystery. There are many mysteries that humans have to participate in like children because they are so big that they don't really understand them, and that is one of them. Forgiveness. It's a big one. Thank you.

APPENDIX B

from the Sacramento Bee
Monday, February 21, 2000
Page A7

New cells in brain? Heads nodding 'yes'

by Edie Lau
Bee Science Writer

WASHINGTON – No more excuses about dead brain cells allowed. The dogma that people are born with all the neurons they will ever possess is utterly turned on its head.

Even the fellow who is widely cited as tamping that dogma into place 15 years ago with a study on the limits in primates of making new brain cells says now that he was misunderstood.

"I was misquoted as saying, 'Read my lips: No new neurons,'" said Pasko Rakic, a developmental biologist at Yale University in New Haven, Conn. "I didn't say no, I said limits."

Having fun with the turn of history, the professor of neuroscience told an audience of fellow scientists this weekend that he's been accused by his 80-year-old aunt Maria of being a pessimist. "Pasko," she asked, "why are you staying in my way to get new neurons?"

Aunt Maria would have liked hearing the session on adult neurogenesis—the making of new brain cells—at the annual meeting of the American Association for the Advancement of Science, which continues this week. She would have heard not only about recent evidence that some brain cells are refreshed even in elderly people but also newer research that suggests scientists can manipulate immature cells to repair parts of the brain that wouldn't naturally be renewed.

She would also have seen new life given to old work by Fernando Nottebohm, a neuroscientist and bird-watcher who, during the same period that Rakic looked fruitlessly for brain-cell growth in monkeys, found that parts of the canary brain are reborn seasonally, enabling the birds to learn new songs each year.

Nottebohm, a researcher at Rockefeller University in New York City, remembers giving a talk to scientists in 1985 about new hope for neurology. People didn't listen as respectfully in those days. "I was in the minority then," he said. "Now I'm part of a very (large) club.

The "club" draws more significance today from Nottebohm's discovery that cells in parts of the male canary brain die off in spring as breeding season begins and are replenished in fall, helping the birds learn a fresh musical repertoire for courtship the next year. Nottebohm believes the old cells must die to make room physically for the new ones.

He also found that the birds that exercised their new brain cells by singing retained those cells longer. Birds whose songs were interrupted—by a researcher waving his hands—produced less of a particular chemical that advances cell growth and survival. "The more you use a circuit, the more you promote cell survival," Nottebohm said.

Conceptually, that finding jibes with recent research by Fred Gage at the Salk Institute in La Jolla that mice that run grew more brain cells and retained them longer. Gage also has found that brain cells survived better in mice given an "enriched" environment consisting of more cage space, a running wheel and a tunnel like those given to pet hamsters.

It was Gage and collaborators who made the revolutionary announcement in the fall of 1998 that even adult humans grow new brain cells. This they discovered by studying the brains of five Swedish cancer patients ages 55 to 75. Three weeks to two years before their deaths, the patients were injected with chemicals that mark dividing cells. Later, the researchers found the markers that indicated that immature brain cells were proliferating and producing new neurons.

Gage said Saturday that scientists know of only two sites in the brain that produce new cells. One is in the dentate gyrus, a portion of the hippocampus, which controls learning and short-term memory. The other, deep inside the brain, is called the subventricular zone.

But it's possible that the source of a new cell does not determine its fate in the brain as much as its environment. Gage said his lab has found that immature cells from the spinal cord grafted to the hippocampus can give rise to new neuronal cells. Even more fantastically, spinal stem cells imported to an adult optic nerve took on the characteristics of optic nerve cells.

Rakic, though now an avowed believer in neurogenesis, said there may be good reason that humans evolved to be born with most of the 100 billion neurons they will ever have. "In evolution, we traded the ability to 'regenerate neurons for the ability to retain them," he said. "Unlike birds, we don't need to learn a new song every year. . . . For (long-term) memory, it would be a disadvantage. These cells didn't go to college. We could maybe work on another approach—how to preserve (existing) cells."

Then he offered his version of President John F. Kennedy's famous saying, "Ask not what new neurons can do for you. Ask what you can do for your old neurons."

On Sunday, Paula Tallal described research about just that—helping existing neurons to function better. Co-director of the Center for Molecular and Behavioral Neuroscience, Tallal has helped develop a computer program that helps children overcome language disabilities. Essentially, the children's brains are slow to hear subtle differences between sounds—the difference between ball and doll, for instance.

The software slows the sound so that the child can hear the difference, then slowly speeds up the enunciation as the child catches on. As, with muscles trained to lift weights, the brain can be trained to overcome weaknesses.

Tallal acknowledged that the concept behind this is not new, although the exercise is. "We've always known that practice makes perfect," she said. Now scientists are beginning to understand why.

APPENDIX C

Dennis Klocek is Director of the Goethean Studies Program at Rudolf Steiner College. Trained as a painter, he holds an M.F.A. degree from the Tyler School of Art at Temple University and a Waldorf Teacher Education Diploma from Rudolf Steiner College. He taught for nine years at Brookdale Community College in New Jersey and has studied broadly in the life sciences, focusing on botany, geology, meteorology and biology. The Goethean approach to science has inspired much of his teaching, writing, and research. He lectures extensively on education, bio-dynamic gardening, inner development, and aspects of Goethean science throughout the United States. He is author of *Drawing from the Book of Nature, Weather and Cosmos, A Bio-Dynamic Book of Moons, Seeking Spirit Vision,* and numerous articles that have appeared in professional journals.

The Goethean Studies Program is a seven-month course based on Goethe's approach to aesthetics and on the work of Rudolf Steiner (1861-1925), philosopher, scientist, and founder of Anthroposophy. Steiner's insights have led to worldwide activities in new forms of architecture, education, medicine, art, philosophy, and agriculture.

The Goethean Studies Program has its roots firmly in the alchemical tradition. The alchemists of old recognized the intimate relationship between the human soul and the natural world. They understood that nature was a "book" of lawful movements and patterns. They also knew that these movements, if perceived accurately, were a map of their own souls. Goethe understood the alchemical quest. To experience the "open secret of nature" as he called it, required a method other than that of the reductionism applied in traditional science. He developed a way of exploring the world that allows one to enter the phenomena as a creative participant, rather than to remain an observer.

Designed to help students to develop enlivened powers of perception, this program offers a daily rhythm of exercises in inner development, science experiments, and practice in the arts. The wonders of the natural world—with focus on the study of botany, meteorology, comparative mythology, and color—are explored through this approach.

References

The following books by Rudolf Steiner have been used in preparing these lectures:

Balance in Teaching. 3d ed. Spring Valley, New York: Mercury Press, 1990.

Fundamentals of Therapy. Spring Valley, New York: Mercury Press, 1999.

An Outline of Esoteric Science (also published under the title *Occult Science: An Outline*). Hudson, New York: Anthroposophic Press, 1997.

The World of the Senses and the World of the Spirit. Vancouver, Canada: Steiner Book Centre, Inc., 1979.